Psychosocial Issues
in the Treatment
of Alcoholism

Psychosocial Issues in the Treatment of Alcoholism

David Cook
Shulamith Lala Ashenberg Straussner
Christine Huff Fewell
Editors

The Haworth Press
New York • London

Psychosocial Issues in the Treatment of Alcoholism has also been published as *Alcoholism Treatment Quarterly*, Volume 2, Number 1, Spring 1985.

The Haworth Press, Inc. 10 Alice Street, Binghamton, NY 13904-1580
EUROSPAN/Haworth, 3 Henrietta Street, London WC2E 8LU England

Library of Congress Cataloging in Publication Data
Main entry under title: .

Psychosocial issues in the treatment of alcoholism.

Has also been issued as Alcoholism treatment quarterly, volume 2, number 1, Spring 1985.
    Includes bibliographical references.
    1. Alcoholism — Treatment — Addresses, essays, lectures. I. Cook, David, 1945- . II. Straussner, Shulamith Lala Ashenberg. III. Fewell, Christine.
HV5275.P75   1985   616.86′106   84-28966
ISBN 0-86656-363-6
ISBN 0-86656-401-2 (pbk.)

Psychosocial Issues in the Treatment of Alcoholism

Alcoholism Treatment Quarterly
Volume 2, Number 1

CONTENTS

Contributors

Flora Colao, M.S.W. Founder, Rape Crisis Program, Department of Community Medicine, St. Vincent's Hospital, New York City.

David Cook, C.S.W. Psychotherapist, Private Practice, New York City. Instructor, Rutgers Summer School of Alcohol Studies, New Brunswick, New Jersey. Co-Chairperson, Publications Committee of the Alcoholism Committee, NASW, New York City Chapter.

Christine Huff Fewell, A.C.S.W. Psychotherapist, Private Practice, Hastings-On-Hudson and New York City. Formerly Social Worker, Smithers Alcohol Treatment and Training Center, St. Luke's-Roosevelt Hospital Center, New York City.

Marian Goldberg, A.C.S.W. Coordinator of Social Work Service of the St. Luke's Hospital Comprehensive Alcoholism Treatment Program, St. Luke's-Roosevelt Hospital Center, New York City. Chairperson-NASW 13th Annual Alcoholism Institute, New York City.

Carole Katz, A.C.S.W. Director of Supervision, Training Analyst, Senior Supervisor, and Faculty, The Institute for Mental Health Education, Englewood, New Jersey. Psychotherapist, Private Practice, New York City.

Valerie R. Levinson, C.S.W. Psychotherapist, Private Practice, New York City. Candidate in Psychoanalysis, Center for Modern Psychoanalytic Studies, New York City. Consultant, Alcoholism Council of Greater New York.

Meryl Nadel, M.S.W. Parent/Child Specialist, Bronx House Jewish Community Center, Bronx, New York.

Margaret Nichols, Ph.D. Director, Institute for Personal Growth, Highland Park, New York City.

Kathy Stillson, A.C.S.W. Director, Nu-Prospect House, the Long Island College Hospital Division of Alcoholism Services; Chairperson, NASW Alcoholism Committee, New York City Chapter; Stress Management Consultant, New York City.

Shulamith Lala Ashenberg Straussner, A.C.S.W. Private Consultant, New York City, Co-Chairperson, Publications Committee of the Alcoholism Committee, NASW, New York City.

Sandra Turner, M.S.W. Chief and Clinical Coordinator, Outreach Component, Women's Program, St. Vincent's Hospital Alcoholism Service, New York City.

Dava L. Weinstein, M.S.W. Private Practice, New York City.

Acknowledgements

The Editors wish to express their appreciation to the following individuals who helped make this book possible: Anne Eglinton, Executive Director, New York City Chapter and Jacqueline Atkins and David Garrity of the National Publication Office of the National Association of Social Workers; Eda Harris and Marian Goldberg who were the chairpersons of the 13th and 14th Annual All Day Alcoholism Institutes respectively; and to Dan Alan Hirsch and Robert Shiesley for the use of their Personal Computers.

Psychosocial Issues in the Treatment of Alcoholism

Introduction

David Cook, C.S.W.
Shulamith Lala Ashenberg Straussner, A.C.S.W.
Christine Huff Fewell, A.C.S.W.

Pessimism about alcoholics and their amenability to treatment has been the prevailing attitude among health professionals until recent years. Historically, controversy has surrounded the etiology of alcoholism and the best way to approach its treatment. When Alcoholics Anonymous (AA) was established in 1935 and began to be successful, the medical profession was amazed. Heretofore medical-psychiatric theories had provided little in the way of practical approaches to alcoholism treatment.[1] It was in this climate that E. M. Jellenik did his first major work on the phenomenology of alcoholism in 1946.[2] The data for this work was obtained from a questionnaire designed by alcoholics and circulated to 98 members by the official publication of Alcoholics Anonymous, the AA Grapevine. It was later administered to 2,000 more members of AA and the data from these questionnaires was published in 1952 in Jellenik's now classic work, "The Phases of Alcohol Addiction."[3] Jellenik's disease concept paved the way for the medical profession in this country to view alcoholism as a disease and thereby include it in the legitimate province of medicine, thus acting against the oldest stereotype of alcoholism—that it was a moral problem and its victims were suffering from lack of will power.[4] Alcoholism now met the medical criteria for a disease by having a set of identifiable symptoms, a predictable course and a systematic treatment process. The fourth criteria, its etiology, is still inadequately understood.

The single most important identifiable symptom of alcoholism was loss of control which marked the beginning of the disease process. This loss of control meant that the alcoholic could not predict when he would stop drinking or when he would start drinking and

Collection of original papers presented at the Thirteenth and Fourteenth Annual NASW Alcoholism Institutes sponsored by the Alcoholism Committee of the New York City Chapter of the National Association of Social Workers.

1

thus pointed to abstinence as the ideal goal for treatment. The goal of abstinence as the primary treatment focus led to a divergence from the psychoanalytic treatment goals which viewed alcoholism as a symptom of an underlying disorder. Since at that time the social work mainstream had a generally psychoanalytic orientation, social workers were as frustrated as other psychodynamically-oriented professionals with the alcoholic's poor prognosis for recovery via psychoanalytic treatment methods.

It was the lack of success with this population that limited the interest and involvement of all the mental health professionals. The recent growth of alcoholism treatment programs in which social workers and other mental health professionals work together with alcoholism counselors who have become familiar with the teachings of Alcoholics Anonymous has led to an exciting new trend in which mental health professionals are beginning to integrate their unique training and skills with the successful methods derived from the disease concept and the teachings of AA. Such interdisciplinary collaboration has led to the integration of alcoholism treatment into the mainstream of social work practice as well as enriching the alcoholism field.

The origin of today's highly successful specialized alcoholism treatment facilities can be traced to the establishment of the Yale Plan Clinics at New Haven and Hartford, Connecticut, under the sponsorship of the Connecticut Prison Association and the Laboratory of Applied Physiology of Yale University. These clinics, established in March, 1944, appear to be the first ones in the country in which professional social workers worked alongside physicians and psychiatrists, under the direction of a recovered alcoholic.[5]

Today, thousands of social workers are involved and contribute to all aspects of the rapidly growing field of alcoholism: their involvement ranges from alcoholism prevention to treatment; from program development to administration; from policy planning to research. Their practice concerns deal both with the intrapsychic as well as the psycho-social aspects of alcohol misuse and alcoholism.

This wide range of interests and theoretical perspectives is reflected in the presentation of the yearly Alcoholism Institute of the New York City Chapter of the National Association of Social Workers. One of the earliest efforts to recognize alcoholism treatment as a specialized area of social work practice came from Margaret Bailey, author of *Alcoholism and Family Casework; Theory and Prac-*

tice.[6] The Alcoholism Committee was organized by Dr. Bailey in 1967 and one of their earliest efforts was to offer training via an Alcoholism Institute, first held in 1969. The Institutes have continued to the present, growing in size and sophistication. One of the Institutes' major focuses has been to help social workers adapt their more generic and psychodynamic training to the needs of the alcoholism field by providing specialized information.

As the Institutes grew, offering more and more workshops, an effort began to make this information, which was often both innovative and original, more widely available. The first effort was a special issue of *Social Casework*[7] published in 1978 and composed of six papers presented at the Ninth Annual Institute. The following year a special issue of *Health and Social Work*[8] devoted to alcohol problems, contained six more papers from the Tenth Annual Institute. Fourteen papers presented at the Eleventh and Twelfth Annual Institutes were published in a book by the Rutgers Center of Alcohol Studies entitled *Social Work Treatment of Alcohol Problems.*[9] The current volume represents the fourth publication of papers presented at the Thirteenth and Fourteenth Institutes and is a random sampling of some of the issues facing practitioners today.

The integration of the behavioral approach and the psychodynamic approach is particularly clearly elucidated in Valerie Levinson's paper, "The Compatibility of the Disease Concept with a Psychodynamic Approach in the Treatment of Alcoholism." She describes its particular value in developing a treatment strategy with individuals presenting themselves at non-alcohol specific treatment agencies with problems other than alcoholism. The approach described allows for the reframing of the alcohol problem from a symptom of an underlying problem to the problem itself. She then moves into an examination of the psychic forces which are at play within the individual and their ability to enhance or interfere with sobriety.

One such psychic force is resistance, a phenomenon well known to all mental health practitioners. Addressing it and working it through is one of the first and most crucial steps in any treatment. In alcoholism treatment it has a unique role since no treatment can take place while someone is actively alcoholically drinking. Yet the inability or resistance to stopping drinking is the presenting problem. Dava Weinstein describes several strategic treatment techniques in alcoholism treatment which are valuable tools for dealing with resistances in her paper by the same name. These include reframing, time-limited treatment, going slow to get going, and using metaphors.

Alcoholics frequently have difficulty dealing with intense feelings, specifically those relating to loss, and often use alcohol to assuage the anxiety brought on by these feelings. The paper by Goldberg on "Loss and Grief: Major Dynamics in the Treatment of Alcoholism," shows how by using the loss of alcohol itself in early sobriety as the first major dynamic to surmount, the ego is strengthened for further grief work. A model for treatment is outlined beginning with a contract with the individual or group which outlines the tasks of therapy. Through the process of taking a detailed history, exploring how alcohol is given up, exploring memories of the lost drinking experiences, understanding the meaning and function of alcohol during the progression of alcoholism and in exploring the effects associated with all of these things, resolution of the loss is facilitated.

Sexuality is usually ignored in alcoholism treatment programs but is often an issue about which patients are secretly very concerned. "The Integration of Sexuality into Alcoholism Treatment" by Christine Fewell points out that while timing of more detailed intervention in sexual issues often should be postponed until sobriety is well established, there are diagnostic issues which are important to sobriety such as the role sexual conflicts played in the alcoholism. In addition to gathering information about sexual functioning from patients, there is a need to give information to them. A sample educational lecture based on a review of the literature on alcoholism and sexuality is outlined.

Until the mid-1970s, the literature on alcohol misuse and alcoholism among women was scarce. Since then, however, alcoholism, as well as the whole area of substance abuse in women has been receiving increasing recognition from all of the helping professions, including social workers. In line with the growing recognition of this problem population, this volume presents three papers which focus on women, and one paper which deals with the impact of maternal drinking on their offspring.

In her chapter on "Alcoholism in Women: Current Knowledge and Implications for Treatment," Straussner provides an overview of the current state of knowledge regarding alcoholism in women, and points out that alcoholism in women differs not only from alcoholism in men, but that alcoholic women differ greatly from each other. Thus, it is important that these differences be recognized and addressed in the diagnoses and treatment of alcoholic women, as well as in future research.

A different, somewhat more controversial, perspective of substance abuse among women is offered by Nichols in her paper "Theoretical Concerns in the Clinical Treatment of Substance-Abusing Women: A Feminist Analysis." It is Dr. Nichols' contention that the roots of female alcohol and prescription drug misuse lie in the sociopolitical arena in which sexism and oppression of women exists. Successful treatment of women, she asserts, requires an understanding of these forces and necessitates the changing of women's role in society.

In an examination of "Alcoholism and Sexual Assault: A Treatment Approach for Women Exploring Both Issues," the authors who similarly identify themselves as feminists, approach the issue initially from a peer support perspective. They explore the issues of women who have either been incest or rape victims as well as being alcoholic. In spite of their initial treatment design, Colao and Turner discovered that their group members virtually forced them into more traditionally therapeutic roles by expressing transferential issues which recreated the feelings about the family system involving the original trauma.

Social workers and other treatment professionals need not only be aware of the possible etiology and the impact of alcoholism on women, but must also be familiar with the potential impact of alcohol upon the offspring of drinking women. To that end, Nadel, in her article "Offspring With Fetal Alcohol Effects: Identification and Intervention," provides an overview of Fetal Alcohol Effects and Fetal Alcohol Syndrome and discusses both preventive and appropriate intervention strategies.

In the alcoholism field the need to be aware of countertransference and burn-out on the part of the treatment staff is particularly acute due to the nature of denial and impulsive behavior in chronic alcoholism. The paper by Stillson and Katz on "A Supervisory Group Process Approach to Address Staff Burnout and Countertransference in Alcoholism Treatment," discusses some of the causes of these problems plaguing treatment staff. A clinical excerpt from a group with alcoholism treatment staff is presented together with comments on the interventions of the co-leaders which illustrates a method of mediating and resolving these countertransferential feelings so that the therapist is able to respond creatively to the patients' needs.

The papers described above do not, by any means, offer a comprehensive picture of the psychosocial issues involved in alcoholism treatment. They do, however, address some of the most relevant treatment issues which can be found in alcoholism literature today.

REFERENCES

1. Keller, Mark, "On the Loss-of-Control Phenomenon in Alcoholism," *British Journal of Addictions*, Vol. 67, pp. 153-166, 1972.

2. Jellenik, E. M., "Phases in the Drinking History of Alcoholics: Analysis of a Survey Conducted by the Official Organ of Alcoholics Anonymous," *Quarterly Journal of Studies on Alcohol*, 1946, Vol. 7, No. 1, pp. 1-88.

3. Jellenik, E. M., "Phases of Alcohol Addiction," *Quarterly Journal of Studies on Alcohol*, Vol. 13, No. 4, pp. 673-684, Dec. 1952.

4. King, Barbara, Bissell, LeClair, & Holding, Eileen, "The Usefulness of the Disease Concept in Working with Wives of Alcoholics," *Social Work in Health Care*, Vol. 3, pp. 443-455, Summer, 1978.

5. Greene, Marian Schemer, "The Role of Social Workers in the Treatment of Alcoholism," Masters Dissertation, The New York School of Social Work, Columbia University, June 1946.

6. Bailey, Margaret, DSW, *Alcoholism and Family Casework: Theory and Practice*, New York City Affiliate, Inc., National Council on Alcoholism, New York City, 1968.

7. Family Service Association of America, "Dimensions of Alcoholism Treatment," *Social Casework*, Vol. 59, No. 1, Jan 1978.

8. National Association of Social Workers, *Health and Social Work*, Vol. 4, No. 4, Nov 1979.

9. Cook, David, Fewell, Christine, & Riolo, John, *Social Work Treatment of Alcohol Problems*, Rutgers Center of Alcohol Studies, New Brunswick, New Jersey, 1983.

The Compatibility
of the Disease Concept
With a Psychodynamic Approach
in the Treatment of Alcoholism

Valerie R. Levinson, C.S.W.

ABSTRACT. Controversy exists regarding treatment approaches to alcoholism. The disease model or the psychodynamic model have been advocated as though they were mutually exclusive. This paper discusses how both can be utilized. The focus on alcoholism as a disease helps the patient to view his addiction as something to be arrested and managed, not understood/rationalized. However, psychodynamic formulations are necessary to develop an individualized treatment plan to resolve the patient's resistances to availing himself of the help Alcoholics Anonymous and alcoholism therapy have to offer. Some characteristic resistances, and techniques used to resolve them, are offered.

PURPOSE

There has been some confusion and even disagreement in the alcoholism treatment field as to when and how to use a disease concept approach and when to use psychodynamic understanding and formulations in treatment. In some ways, they seem contradictory, *psychodynamic* implying an intrapsychic orientation and *disease concept* implying a more behavioral approach. Nevertheless, they are not only compatible, but also complementary in treatment and can be used in combination. This paper is a beginning effort at integration of the two approaches to treatment.

It is possible to use a more single minded disease concept orientation when a person comes into treatment in an alcoholism facility. When the patient says, "I'm not alcoholic," one can always wonder aloud about how he got referred here. But when the individual comes to an outpatient psychiatric clinic, a family agency, or a private practice setting with a presenting problem of depression and the therapist picks up that the problem is alcohol abuse and confronts the patient with the diagnosis too quickly, there is a good chance that the patient will leave treatment. The goal is to keep the patient engaged while maintaining a focus on the alcoholism. It may be necessary to move more slowly in treatment in a non-alcoholism facility than in an alcoholism facility.

FORMAT

This paper concerns a circumscribed phase of treatment, which will be described. Basic principles of alcoholism treatment which are assumed throughout this paper will be listed. *Disease concept* will be defined, and the rationale for its use and implications for treatment will be given. Finally, the *psychodynamic* approach will be defined and a number of psychodynamic issues will be discussed with illustrative case examples. Some dynamically-oriented treatment techniques which have been found to be helpful are included.

PHASE OF TREATMENT

The focus is on the initial phase of treatment in the context of the outpatient setting. This general treatment approach applies to any given patient population. In this phase the patient may have acknowledged the problem but still only pay lip service to it. The person may even say, "I know I can't drink," but is resistant to attending AA or going for detoxification. See Zimberg[1] for a description of stages in increased identification as an alcoholic.

BASIC ASSUMPTIONS

There are certain principles of alcoholism treatment which are assumed in this paper.

— Until the alcoholism has been arrested, other problems cannot be completely resolved as they will get worse as the drinking, or use of other mood changers, gets worse.
— The therapist takes an active stance in educating the patient about the effects of alcohol and the illness of alcoholism.

—AA has been found to be the most effective tool in helping people stay sober.

—People are not seen in sessions if they are high. Although they may still be actively drinking outside, they must be sober for twenty-four hours in order to have a session. If they are unable to remain alcohol free for twenty-four hours the appropriate treatment is probably a medical detoxification in the hospital. Otherwise there is the danger that the person will go into withdrawal. And talking therapy with someone who is addicted and in need of detoxification is useless as the person's thoughts and feelings are too clouded by the alcohol.

For further elaboration, see Levinson and Straussner,[2] Fewell and Bissel,[3] Weinberg,[4] and Petty.[5]

THE DISEASE CONCEPT APPROACH

Definition

The disease concept, as propounded by Dr. E.M. Jellinek,[6] refers to the fact that alcoholism is recognizable by a cluster of symptoms regardless of the patient's lifestyle, personality, upbringing, level of pathology, social class, education, or other psychosocial variable. It is diagnosable as a disease at the point at which the habitual use of alcohol has caused damage in some area of the person's life, be it the physical, social, work, psychological or spiritual. Some of the markers of the disease are the presence of increased tolerance to alcohol; inability to control the amount of liquor ingested at a given time or inability to remain abstinent; craving and compulsion related to drinking; and of course the presence of withdrawal symptoms indicating physical addiction, such as insomnia, sweats, tremors, nausea and vomiting. There may be physical and genetic predispositions to becoming alcoholic. A more complete enumeration of symptoms and elucidation of the part they play in the disease may be found in Jellinek,[7] Levinson and Straussner,[8] Levinson,[9] and Fewell et al.[10]

Implications for Treatment

Viewing alcoholism as a disease as opposed to a symptom of underlying psychopathology leads one to approach its treatment with behavioral techniques. The patient is taught how to cope with the disease. The patient is held responsible for cooperating with treatment and making an effort to recover, but not responsible for having the illness. Even though the patient may wish to understand his or her pathology as a way of making the pain go away, the approach is to change behavior, not to understand reasons, in order to cope better. Patients are surprised to find that they do feel much better when the behavior is changed, regardless of what they understand at that point.

The disease concept redefines the problem as a systems problem.[11] It is the person in relation to the disease and the environment rather than an intrapsychic problem.

The therapist models the new point of view for the patient by making it clear that therapy alone will not arrest alcoholism. AA is the appropriate treatment for arresting the disease. At the stage at which the person is still actively drinking, addiction is not dealt with as a psychodynamic issue. Therapy is primarily educational and is offered as a way of helping the person get to AA or to an inpatient alcoholism program.

In 1945, in *The Psychoanalytic Theory of Neurosis*, Otto Fenichel[12] wrote:

> There is still much contention over the psychoanalytic therapy of persons with morbid impulses or addictions. An understanding of the mechanisms involved makes it plain that in principle such patients are amenable to psychoanalytic treatment, but that from a practical point of view there are particular problems to be overcome . . .
>
> The best time to begin an analysis is obviously during or immediately after withdrawal. But it is not to be expected that the patient will remain abstinent throughout the analysis. If he has an opportunity he will probably use the drug again whenever the resistance in his analysis predominates. This is the reason why addicts are to be analyzed in institutions rather than as ambulatory patients . . .
>
> *Through a certain type of preliminary treatment,* [emphasis is mine] it may be possible to increase the patient's awareness that he is ill, and to strengthen his wish to be cured, before psychoanalysis proper begins; and a certain activity on the part of the analyst, . . . may be necessary in dealing with the intolerance of tension and the tendency to "act out." (pp. 385–386)

The patient incorrectly thinks he has to understand his drinking because he believes the disease is part of his psychological make-up; the disease is equated with the person's self, rather than being a syndrome about which he can learn.

The kinds of arrangements a person might make to accommodate to the recovery from the disease might be avoiding situations which tap the temptation to drink; to think through problem situations in advance and plan a coping strategy before the event occurs; to educate people in the social network as to how one would like to be treated, such as not offering drinks. A whole additional repertoire of coping mechanisms is available through the collective expertise of AA members. In AA the member is asked to take the first step, or admit he is powerless over alcohol, and to surrender. Bateson[13] analyzes the process as follows: surrender implies giving up the false notion of a duality between a conscious will or self and the remainder of the personality. It resolves a fallacious split. The patient's wish to understand is an effort to maintain control rather than to define oneself as an addict who is powerless. The person who surrenders changes the system by which he relates to the world; "The change is toward a knowledge of the interdependence of man and nature rather than a persistence of the view that man is master of all" (King,[14] p. 190).

The notion of willpower is a mistaken conception of the problem. Use of willpower, which is disparaged in AA, is no more possible than lifting oneself by one's bootstraps.

THE PSYCHODYNAMIC APPROACH TO TREATMENT

Psychodynamic refers to the interplay of psychic and energic forces. A psychodynamic orientation would include the assessment of the person's premorbid ability to cope as well as assessment of the current state of mechanisms for coping, that is, the status secondary to alcoholism; including the erosion or strength of such ego functions as judgment, memory and concentration. The assessment would also include the kinds of defenses the person employs, the developmental level the person has achieved (or regressed to), the individual's own unique history, and how these all impact on each other. Some psychodynamic issues characteristic of people with alcoholism follow.

Compliance

The patient acknowledges his or her alcoholism and the necessity of doing something about it. There is the unspoken message: "I feel I can't do what you're suggesting; I can't stop; I can't make it to an AA meeting; I know you're right but . . ." At the time he promises to go to AA, for example, it feels real, but the resolve quickly crumbles. Complying postpones dealing with the drinking. The patient eludes a trap of feeling obligated and committed. He avoids conflict with the therapist and with his own superego. Intentions are voiced and plans made according to what feels right at the moment and dropped when they don't feel right in the next moment.

The therapist has the problem of how long to go on treating a compliant person whose addiction has not been arrested. It is possible to give an ultimatum such as, "It is unethical for me to continue treating you because your drinking is getting worse. AA (or rehabilitation) is the appropriate help; call me for your next appointment only after you have been to a meeting (or gone to rehabilitation)." That may be the last the therapist may see of the patient. The therapist's conflict is on the one hand not to be a participant in the alcoholism by providing treatment that cannot work. On the other hand, there may be the possibility that continuing the relationship while the patient's tension builds and crises escalate will enable the patient to get to AA or rehabilitation sooner than if he left treatment to continue to drink.

Need for Control

The wish to maintain a sense of control can interfere with the alcoholic's becoming involved in AA. When in a meeting members speak of The First Step (admitting they are powerless over alcohol and that their lives have become unmanageable), and about acceptance and surrender, the patient may feel threatened. To the person new in treatment and AA, to accept that he has the disease of alcoholism may be equated with being a passive person who is submitting to someone else's authority. H.M. Tiebout[15] speaks to

> the need to distinguish between submission and surrender. In submission, an individual accepts reality consciously but not unconsciously. He accepts as a practical fact that he cannot at that moment conquer reality, but lurking in his unconscious is

the feeling, "there'll come a day"—which implies no real acceptance and demonstrates conclusively that the struggle is still going on. With submission, which at best is a superficial yielding, tension continues. When, on the other hand, the ability to accept reality functions on the unconscious level, there is no residual battle, and relaxation ensues with freedom from strain and conflict. In fact, it is perfectly possible to ascertain to what extent the acceptance of reality is on the unconscious level by the degree of relaxation which develops. The greater the relaxation, the greater is the inner acceptance of reality. (p.3)

Therefore, it must be made clear that he may choose from AA and from the treatment only what applies. The individual is still in control and in charge. At this stage in the treatment, the patient may need to be reassured that he does not have to give up his or her entire life, or value system, or identity to AA (although it may be that once the person does become involved and has less conflict about control, he will choose to immerse himself in the program).

A young executive prided himself on his ability to do the impossible and enjoyed rising to the challenge. He had many criticisms of AA. He had been taught not to complain, that his negative reactions were generally about insignificant details and that he should only verbalize things that were significant. He agreed to attend a meeting only after he was given an assignment I "doubted he would be able to carry out." The task was to attend several meetings, pay attention only to details about which he felt critical, and bring his criticisms back into the session. Prior to his assignment he was almost incapable of expressing his negative feelings about AA. He rose to this challenge, however, and successfully completed his assignment. I supported all his criticisms. He requested and received more similar assignments but began to report increasingly positive responses to meetings.

Denial of Dependency Needs

Most alcoholics cannot tolerate feelings of inadequacy, helplessness or impotence. So before they have accepted being alcoholic, they act as if they are omnipotent. Hence the phrase AA adopted from Freud: "His majesty, the baby."

This omnipotence, or denial of dependency needs is the most powerful resistance throughout the treatment. It originates in the period in which the infant denied its helplessness. If the parent were indeed neglectful or abusive, then for today's grown child to give up the defense of omnipotence would be to get in touch with the feeling that his or her survival is in peril.

The idea of coming for treatment can be humiliating for the alcoholic person who wants to have the feeling he can handle the problem alone. The idea of going to AA is even worse because it usually means to the person that not only is he not managing independently, but that he is entrusting himself to peers. The alcoholic tends to feel contempt for peers (unconsciously projecting his own self hate onto the others). The striving to look independent is a reaction formation to unfulfilled dependence. The patient has most often experienced rejection by parents when he was in need as a child. Frequently one or both parents were alcoholic.

> An alcoholic one year sober in AA came for therapy to work on relationship issues. He said his problem was that he was very possessive. As a child he had been very possessive as well. He used to cry and cry for his mother. He reported that to break him of his possessiveness his mother would hide in the closet so he couldn't find her. He did not seem to think his mother might have behaved any differently, perceiving himself to be at fault. He grew up internalizing enormous frustration, felt very needy, and assumed it was futile to try to get his needs met.

The therapist must understand and resolve the resistance to asking for help, to trusting, to letting the therapist in, to developing a working partnership. The major resistance as discussed above is the alcoholic's reluctance to ask for help. In fact, on one alcoholism agency's intake form one of the dispositions to be checked off, in addition to such items as "AA, psychiatric treatment, rehabilitation, group, etc." was "DIM," or, "Do It Myself!" Historically, the stage is set for this problem when the infant cries in pain or hunger and the mother responds inconsistently or not at all. The child does not learn that if it makes its needs known, the mother will respond in a predictable way. All the child experiences is having urgent unmet needs and the corresponding rage which floods an ego not sufficiently developed to channel the rage. Hence the need in later life to do something about feelings rather than to verbalize them or ask for help with them.

Today's alcoholic who grew up in an alcoholic household no doubt had the experience as a child that when he had questions the parents responded as if there were only a right or wrong answer. Or if the child had fears or problems or attacked the parent's behavior, the parent was likely to respond defensively. There was a good chance the parent would retaliate against the child verbally, or, if things got heated, physically, even violently. The child missed the opportunity of an ongoing discussion which would generate alternatives and compromises.

If the patient can be trained to bring the therapist in, that kind of contact will be generalizable to others. In AA, the patient will be in more of a position to let the group help.

> For example, the patient may come in and talk on and on about what is bothering him without getting any resolution. The problem is just thrown out into the air. The therapist who tries to go ahead and help may find the patient does not seem to want help; at least the help may be falling on deaf ears. In this case, the therapist may wait a while and then say, "You know, you've talked about this for some time and I know it's bothering you. I'm wondering how come you haven't asked for any of my ideas about it?" Or, "Have you thought of asking for my help with this?" The patient has the option of ignoring the question or changing the subject, thus nonverbally answering the question, or of beginning the process of learning to ask for help.
>
> The process may take a long time. It might begin something like this:
>
> Therapist: Is there any reason you haven't asked for help with this?
>
> Patient: How can you help? You can't solve my problems.
>
> T: How do you know when you haven't tried me?
>
> P: I have to do it myself.
>
> T: If you could have, you would have already. (or) Isn't that like asking yourself to create something out of nothing? (or) You mean you're supposed to have all the answers?
>
> P: I just need more money. You'd have to give me money.
>
> T: Is the only way I can help you to give you money? Might there be another way?

P: What?

T: Can you tell me what is keeping you from getting more money? (or) Just what is the problem with your finances?

The ensuing interchange will zero in on the nature of the problem with money. The patient learns through the dialogue that solutions can be reached as a result of mutual questioning, brainstorming together, and with his sharing more information.

Most patients enjoy and understand the analogy to the baby's needs to be helped, taught by parents how to do things. One is not brought into this world knowing how to change one's own diaper, after all, or to feed oneself, or know what is dangerous, until taught.

To the extent the patient is genuinely able to ask for help, he is likely to be successful in recovery.

Guilt

As oblivious to the problem as the alcoholic may appear, he only denies and minimizes to the degree he is in conflict between wanting to continue drinking and simultaneously hating himself for it.

A woman came in with the presenting problem of her 12 year old daughter's acting out. Although the woman was in a rage about the daughter's behavior, she was vague as to exactly what the daughter did that was so bad. She focussed on the child as the problem, while she herself was an active alcoholic. Her husband had divorced her and was remarried. Obviously, one of the reasons the child was having trouble was that she had an alcoholic mother. Her mother's personality changed each night and weekend; she was unreliable, irritable, sometimes explosive, sometimes withdrawn. The mother's rage and bitterness regarding her child was her way of avoiding her own responsibility. As long as she could blame, she did not have to feel the depression, anxiety and guilt she would feel if she acknowledged the effect her drinking was having on her child.

Avoiding Intimacy

Intimate relationships arouse feelings of closeness, dependency, frustration, vulnerability, disappointment and loss of identity. The alcoholic is likely to want to avoid these feelings. In treatment, the therapist has to be careful to give the patient the right amount of distance. The therapist who likes to foster a cozy mutual admiration society may have a problem with the alcoholic. The patient may leave, feeling threatened, or intruded on, by the attempts at closeness. (See below for discussion of too much distance.) I have found that many patients seem to feel most comfortable at the beginning with a more businesslike approach.

One way to establish a clear set of boundaries in the relationship is through the use of last names. Sometimes, however, use of last names may pose a problem in that in alcoholism facilities and in AA first names are used. It could feel rejecting to the patient to insist on use of last names. However, if it is not too frustrating, it can be helpful. Most patients are satisfied with the explanation that the use of last names symbolizes the fact that the relationship is special, professional, and will not go beyond the bounds of talking, no matter what is said or what feelings emerge. Roles stay clear even though the patient may wish the therapist to change into a parent, friend or AA sponsor.

Impulsiveness

It is more helpful to treat the patient's impulsiveness as a function of a defect in the ego than as acting out (in which ego controls are better developed but undermined by defensive operations—for elaboration on this concept and on treatment of impulsive patients, see Goldwater).[16] The therapist works to support and build the ego. That is why alternative methods of coping are suggested rather than analyzing what feeling is being acted upon. The patient is accustomed to dealing with feelings by taking an action. That is all he knows. So to suggest stopping and thinking before picking up a drink or doing some other self-destructive action is to suggest something quite foreign and difficult. Education is offered that the patient may attain more control if he uses the phone before the binge starts, writes down thoughts and feelings instead of drinking, practices relaxation techniques, drinks a substitute nonalcoholic beverage, eats something, or delays drinking for a few minutes.

Crenshaw,[17] in her book, *End of the Rainbow*, tells how her counselor helped her handle her impulses to act precipitously:

> I spent an hour with Anna, going over all the aspects of my new life at home. It was, it seemed, going to be very new. New and possibly frightening. My reactions to things were not going to be the same as they had been . . . . I was not, repeat,

not, under any circumstance to make any changes in my life at this time. But, I interrupted, I didn't think I could stay with Alan. I didn't think he wanted me, he wasn't ready to marry me, I was tired of wasting my time, and besides, he drank.

No, I was not to leave Alan at this time.

"But I hate my apartment and I want to move."

"You cannot move at this time."

"But I'm uncomfortable in my apartment. I have a sofa I can't even sit on!"

"You'll give the sofa to charity and take a tax loss."

Anna had practical answers for everything. She warned me all would be lost if I shook up my life just now. Everything was to come to a standstill for one whole year. By then — just maybe then — I would have my head together enough to make rational decisions. (p. 230)

Education is another ego building technique. Educating the patient about feelings may also help defuse the feelings and thereby make them less threatening. For example, just informing the patient that anxiety, sexual arousal, sadness and anger are normal feelings that come and go are not dangerous or bad in and of themselves can be reassuring and reduce the need for the patient to condemn himself and bottle them up.

One impetus for the person's impulsive self-destructive drinking may be overwhelming rage which overpowers an ego not strong enough to regulate and channel the feelings. The action can be a defense against suicide or homicide. The patient does not have the capacity to differentiate between a murderous feeling and actually committing murder. Therefore, a person in the initial stages of treatment may be helped not to get into or stay in a situation which provokes intense rage; he may be told to walk away from it. Later in treatment the feelings may be expressed and explored.

A technique for reducing the patient's impulsiveness is not to treat "crises" as crises. Appointments are not changed to accommodate a crisis. (The patient's whole life is a crisis.) Time on phone calls, while permitted, is kept to a minimum and the patient is encouraged to discuss everything in the session. Sesssions begin and end on time. The patient may be counseled to write down what is bothering him. The patient may be asked on the phone whether he thinks he can tolerate the feeling that is propelling him to want to act. Sometimes merely thinking about the feeling results in mastery.

An alcoholic patient, sober in AA about three months, would leave the session about halfway into her time. She was unable to sit still any longer. She was not able to introspect as to what impelled her to flee. She was permitted to leave, and over time, as she became increasingly able to verbalize feelings and memories, was able to stay in the office for longer periods of time.

Another way of fostering control is to prohibit any actions, including smoking, drinking of soda, eating gum or mints, or getting up and walking around the room. All the person does in the office is talk. The first time the patient begins to light up, the therapist may ask if it would be possible for him to hold off. The explanation is given that it is recommended for treatment only to talk in sessions; that the more feelings go into words rather than up in smoke, the more mileage can be gotten from the therapy. However, the patient may also be requested to say he feels like smoking the minute the urge returns. The patient usually interprets the request to mean he can smoke when he wants, but it is further explained that the request was to be taken quite literally, that is, to say, "I feel like it now." The purpose is to begin to help the patient put all impulses into words. The purpose, in spite of what the patient may think, is not to get him to quit smoking. The process can be generalized to the time when the patient feels like drinking. If he makes a phone call instead, the impulse, being delayed, will die down. While the rule is helpful it can also be used as a goal in therapy for patients who appear not to be able to tolerate it at the beginning. The therapist can be flexible in imposing it, depending on the level of the patient's frustration tolerance. If its seems the patient will feel too explosive if he cannot smoke, he may be asked whether he could wait five, ten, fifteen minutes before lighting up, or whether he could limit smoking to one or two cigarettes in the session. The rule is not intended to be an endurance test for the patient and its use can be negotiated with the patient.

While a certain amount of frustration is necessary for growth, frustration needs to be limited for the alcoholic new to treatment. Sessions should be enjoyable and talking made as easy as possible. The atmosphere should engender enough comfort to keep the flow going. At this stage of treatment interpretations are usually not helpful, being experienced by the patient as attacks rather than aids to understanding. Even if not experienced as an attack, intellectually oriented interpretations fly right over the head of most new alcoholic patients. It is better to gear interventions to promote behavioral change and talking, not necessarily insight. At the beginning, the therapist tries to find a topic, any topic, that the patient can talk about freely, such as sports, politics, the weather, family members—topics which are removed from his or her ego and therefore safe.

A certain amount of non-stimulating self-disclosure of a general nature on the part of the therapist reduces the suspiciousness some patients feel in the presence of a professional.

Unidentified Alcoholism

A patient who is coming to an outpatient setting for the first time and presents with a problem other than alcoholism (but whom the therapist recognizes to be alcoholic) may require slow going. The therapist needs to feel his or her way back and forth between educating the patient regarding the effects of alcohol and following the patient's lead regarding what the patient thinks is the problem. If the patient adamantly denies the problem, the therapist softens educational efforts so as not to get into a power struggle with the patient around the drinking. As trust and a working alliance are developed, the therapist may take more liberties. With a patient in whom the alcoholism is more acceptable, the therapist can move faster. The goal of therapy in either case is to make the drinking ego dystonic.

> A patient came for treatment for insomnia. It soon became clear that she had a serious drinking problem. She was told that drinking alcohol, while seemingly aiding sleep by initially acting as a soporific, actually undermines good sleep by producing the withdrawal effect of agitation when the alcohol wears off a few hours later. The woman scoffed at this notion, replying that she had had a sleep problem since she was a child. I did not argue with her. Nor did I attempt to work on the insomnia as a primary problem. I did suggest that she try a period without alcohol to see what would happen. I also suggested that the patient attend a few AA meetings to learn more about alcohol. The patient became willing to go to AA after several uncontrolled binges which frightened her. The insomnia was not mentioned again.

Externalizing Responsibility for Drinking

The tendency of the patient is to try to get the therapist to argue with him or her about the drinking. The therapist needs to avoid a battle with the patient even though it can be difficult at times.

One way is to take the patient's role by accepting the drinking instead of opposing it, and asking, "Why shouldn't you drink? What's wrong with your drinking?" or "Is this really a problem—I'm not convinced," or "You haven't told me anything that bad about your drinking. What's with your (spouse, boss, friends, etc.) that they're getting on your back?" If the therapist and patient have agreed there is a problem and the patient still anticipates, by projection, that the therapist wants to make him or her stop drinking, the therapist can point out that he or she cannot, will not, and does not wish to control what the patient chooses to do outside the office. If the therapist senses it will be helpful, he or she can even add that the patient has a right to behave suicidally.

Just as the patient is ambivalent about making a commitment to stopping drinking and may try to set the therapist up to take a position so that the patient can resist, so will the patient attempt the same interaction around other issues. The therapist can handle this resistance by *not* asking the patient to make any commitments or promises regarding drinking or even regarding attendance at sessions. The patient is often as ambivalent about coming regularly to sessions as he is to giving up drinking. If that is the case, a short term contract may be made rather than the traditional expectation that the patient show up every week for an indefinite period of time. The efficacy of a short term contract has been discussed by Levinson.[18] If the patient is very ambivalent and the therapist is not at all sure the patient will show again, the therapist suggests that the patient call for the next appointment. Some patients may be more comfortable at the beginning coming every other week. Although the therapist may wonder what can be accomplished with such little contact, it may be that the therapist's willingness to give the patient that much distance will enable the person to continue to come. At a later date the frequency of contact can be increased. A patient can be asked to attend two or three AA meetings "to do research, to observe, not to join or participate" and to report back about his reactions to the meetings. The work of the treatment is on resistance to going once and then on resistance to continuing. Much material will emerge concerning feelings about being alcoholic. Having the freedom in sessions to verbalize all negative feelings about meetings may enable the individual to use the help that is available there. And knowing that he has only agreed to observe a meeting may free the person to attend.

If plans for detoxification or rehabilitation are being discussed, it is helpful for the therapist again not to extract promises regarding date of entry, but to explore feelings about going. Most patients can be put in charge of making the arrangements to go in. The therapist takes more of a waiting stance. The patient takes as much time as needed rather than feeling rushed and reacting by balking at the last minute. Patients, therapists and families can often find themselves feeling a sense of panic because of the patient's chaotic lifestyle and react by acting as if immediate detoxification were a necessity. The reality is that a few more days of drinking are not going to make a difference. The therapist can even slow the patient down, asking if he really thinks he is ready, has he thought of everything he needs to know, has he taken care of everything at home, on the job, or anywhere else? Perhaps the patient can reassure the therapist of his readiness. The therapist anticipates problems, resistance, and tries to elicit all negative feelings and fears. If the therapist allies with the negative side of the patient's ambivalence the patient will not feel he has failed if he does not follow through with the plan. Premature termination of treatment can be avoided.

> Upon returning to outpatient treatment following rehabilitation, a patient spoke disparagingly about the treatment. He claimed he was coming to sessions and to AA because he knew he was supposed to. I tried to sidestep his attempt to make me responsible for his coming by asking about who said he was supposed to come. I explained that as far as I was concerned, I certainly did not feel he had to come to report what AA meetings he was or was not attending. He subsequently expressed interest in making a treatment contract to come every other week.

Ambivalence About AA

AA instills hope and promotes identification with others with the same problem. Consciousness is raised as to the seriousness, pervasiveness and duration of the disease. Identifying with others reduces guilt. Responsibility is shifted away from the self through the member's assuming more dependence on the group. And since AA is a group and not one person, the tendency to resist and defy is lessened. The urge to drink is sublimated through helping others. Techniques are shared to help keep from picking up the first drink. For a therapist's point of view on what AA does, see Bean[19] and Kinney and Montgomery.[20]

The patient who is resistant to attending meetings can be asked what he thinks a meeting would be like. Misconceptions are elicited.

> One woman worried about members proselytizing. She was asked how she might handle anyone who did push her toward getting more involved than she wished. She decided she could say she was just there to listen. If someone asked for her number, she could give a wrong number. (She did not think she could just say no.) Her worst fear about what could happen in AA reflected what she disliked most about her current relationships—she always felt pushed around and could not say no. Some pointers on remaining inconspicuous relieved her anxiety enough for her to make a meeting.

CONCLUSION

It is possible to achieve an integration of the disease concept approach to alcoholism treatment with psychodynamic understanding. The individualized psychodynamic formulation is made to help the therapist gear interventions toward the patient's becoming engaged in treatment, developing a working alliance, making the drinking ego dystonic, and getting to AA for help stopping drinking. The disease concept is used to help the person become interested in maintaining sobriety by adapting behavior to arrest the disease. No insight is needed at this stage of treatment. Understanding reasons for drinking or for other life problems comes later in the treatment, after solid sobriety has been achieved.

REFERENCES

1. Zimberg, Sheldon, "Principles of Alcoholism Psychotherapy," in Zimberg, Sheldon, Wallace, John, and Blume, Sheila, eds., *Practical Approaches to Alcoholism Psychotherapy*, New York: Plenum Press, 1978, pp. 13-15.

2. Levinson, Valerie R. and Straussner, Shulamith L.A., "Social Workers as 'Enablers' in the Treatment of Alcoholics," *Social Casework*, 59, January 1978, pp. 14-20.

3. Fewell, Christine H. and Bissell, LeClair, "The Alcoholic Denial Syndrome: An Alcohol-Focused Approach," *Social Casework*, 59, January 1978, pp. 6-13.

4. Weinberg, Jon, "Counseling Recovering Alcoholics," *Social Work*, July 1973, pp. 84-93.

5. Petty, Mary Lou, "Social Work, the Profession of Choice in the Treatment of Alcoholics," *Journal of the Smith College School of Social Work*, 3, Spring, 1976, pp. 10-15.

6. Jellinek, Elvin M., *The Disease Concept of Alcoholism*, Highland Park, N.J.: Hillhouse Press, 1960.

7. *Ibid.*, pp. 33-45 and pp. 111-149.

8. Levinson and Straussner, *op. cit.* pp. 15-16.

9. Levinson, Valerie R., "How to Conduct an Alcoholism-Focussed Intake: A Verbatim Illustration," *Social Work: Treatment of Alcohol Problems* in the *Treatment Series*, Vol. 5, Edited by Cook, D. Fewell, C. & Riolo J., Rutgers, N.J.: Rutgers Center for Alcohol Studies, 1981.

10. Fewell, Christine, Straussner, Shulamith, Evans, Craig, King, Barbara, Orlin, Alison, and Perone, Frank, "Alcoholism Among Social Workers: Approaching a Colleague with a Drinking Problem," pamphlet published by New York City Chapter, National Association of Social Workers, 1978.

11. King, Barbara, Bissell, LeClair, O'Brien, Peter, "Alcoholics Anonymous, Alcoholism Counseling, and Social Work Treatment," *Health and Social Work*, Vol. 4(4), November 1979, p. 191.

12. Fenichel, Otto, *The Psychoanalytic Theory of Neurosis*, New York: W.W. Norton and Co., 1945, pp. 385-386.

13. Bateson, Gregory, "The Cybernetics of 'Self': A Theory of Alcoholism," in Bateson, *Steps to an Ecology of Mind*, New York: Ballantine Books, 1972, p. 313.

14. King, Barbara, et al., *op. cit.*, p. 190.

15. Tiebout, Harry M., "Surrender Versus Compliance in Therapy with Special Reference to Alcoholism," *Quarterly Journal of Studies on Alcohol*, 14, March 1953, p.3.

16. Goldwater, Eugene, "A Model for Understanding and Treating the Impulsive Patient," *Modern Psychoanalysis*, 1979, p. 189.

17. Crenshaw, Mary Ann, *End of the Rainbow*, New York: Macmillan, 1981, p. 230.

18. Levinson, Valerie R., "The Decision Group: Beginning Treatment in an Alcoholism Clinic," *Health and Social Work*, Vol. 4(4), November, 1979, pp. 205-206.

19. Bean, Margaret, "Alcoholics Anonymous: Expectations of Psychotherapy," *Psychiatric Annals*, March-April, 1975, pp. 45-53.

20. Kinney, Jean and Montgomery, Mary, "Psychotherapy and the Member of Alcoholics Anonymous," in Galanter, Marc, ed., *Currents in Alcoholism*, Vol. 6, New York: Grune & Stratton, 1976, pp. 79-85.

Strategic Treatment Techniques in Alcoholism Treatment: Valuable Tools for Dealing With Resistance

Dava L. Weinstein, M.S.W.

ABSTRACT. This paper illustrates through presentation of theory and clinical examples the applicability of strategic problem-solving therapeutic techniques in the treatment of alcoholism.

THEORETICAL RATIONALE FOR USING STRATEGIC TECHNIQUES IN ALCOHOLISM TREATMENT

The biomedical, social, cultural and genetic issues of alcoholism, course of treatment, recovery process and recidivism are constantly being explored by the health professions.[1] This paper is a continuation of that exploration and its purpose is to draw the clinician's attention to the usefulness of strategic treatment techniques in alcoholism treatment. The research on the pharmacological effects of alcohol on the central nervous system focuses on the sedative-hypnotic effects of the chemical, including decreased cognitive functioning for all persons regardless of status along the continuum from social drinker to end stage alcoholic. Strategic treatment is particularly suited to the special problems of cognitive dysfunctioning resulting from regular alcohol use. These special areas of dysfunction include problem-solving abilities, perceptual-spatial activities and nonverbal abstracting. Verbal functioning remains relatively intact.[2] Strategic techniques are offered to the clinician as particularly effective alcoholism treatment tools given the cognitive dysfunctioning secondary to alcohol abuse for dealing with problems of resistance after the initial identification treatment phase. The tools will be applicable in dealing with early phase alcoholism as well as chronic alcoholism.

Bennett supports the argument for a specific therapeutic approach to individuals who have been regularly under the influence of alcohol:

> *It is important to recognize with cerebral involvement that attitudinal and emotional metacommunications may be all that get through to a person* [italics added]. Poor memory, coupled with a tendency toward literal-mindedness, make it difficult for the person to follow a logical argument . . . It is certain that the counselor who expects a brain-damaged alcoholic to stop drinking solely through sweet reason or guided insight is going to have a long wait. The success of the approach developed by Alcoholics Anonymous undoubtedly is due to the fact that their appeal is not based on logic alone.[3]

The point to be underscored is that *all* persons who take in alcohol experience cerebral dysfunction. That impairment may range from minimal to extensive, from fleeting to permanent. The extent of the dysfunction is dependent on age, gender, number of years drinking, nutritional status, etcetera.[4]

Strategic treatment which is not "based on logic alone" and does not rely on the patient's rational problem-solving potential is a rich resource for the clinician. Strategic practitioners operate on the premise that logical solutions do not always facilitate change, but rather, often compound and perpetuate a problem;[5] and, the view that "psychotherapy is sought not primarily for enlightenment about the unchangeable past but because of dissatisfaction with the present and a desire to better the future."[6]

Take, for example, the person complaining of insomnia. The logical, linear approach to this problem is to try harder to fall asleep. By the time the person has come to treatment s/he (and perhaps the entire family) has tried all sorts of solutions which may take the form of elaborate preparations for sleep. However, persisting in efforts to bring about a spontaneous event (sleep) only disrupts the process further. The instruction to the client to focus on going to bed and staying awake is certainly illogical; yet, clinicians adept at prescribing the symptom see the strategy as invaluable.[7] This example also illustrates the phenomenon that often a solution developed in response to a dilemma becomes a dilemma itself. An example from the alcoholism field would be the partner of an active alcoholic increasing their efforts to help (in this instance, through control) by buying the alcohol for the drinking spouse. In both examples a pattern of behaving in response to a problem has developed. This pattern maintains, rather than alleviates, the unwanted behavior becoming a problem itself.

In order to help individuals and families go beyond the place (repetitive same efforts at problem resolution) they are in it is necessary to look at basic change theory. John Weakland explains that there are parallel components to change. Change brings the desired, hoped for goal as well as some undesired losses: "It is human nature to dig one's heels in resist change."[x] To urge a client/family, through rational discussion and planning, to implement change does not always bring the sought after results. The client/family is alone in the maze of doubts and uncertainties that change would bring, no matter how difficult their present situation.

In this context it is easier to understand the person, aware of his/her chemical dependency and its cost, who continues to refuse alcoholism treatment; or if in treatment, does not use sensible suggestions for change which the professional offers. The alcoholic client is burdened by both his/her natural resistance to change as well as the cognitive dysfunction secondary to alcohol use. The techniques presented in this paper are intended to be used in those treatment situations where direct confrontation and education have not resulted in the client's/family's involvement in recovery.

Strategic therapists, operating from the premise that a person/family becomes stuck trying harder at a planned solution (solution becoming problem)[y] would not use a logical therapeutic approach in such an instance. The strategic therapist would assess the pattern of response to the problem and develop an intervention at a particular point in the pattern based on the theory that a shift in one area of the structure will lead to a reorganization of patterns thus unsticking that situation. The strategies to be presented now are reframing, time-limited treatment, "going slow to get going" and use of metaphors. Anecdotes will illustrate each technique and its efficacy in dealing with resistance to change particular to alcoholism.

REFRAMING

Reframing is that technique in which the clinician takes a totally different posture on the information that the client/family brings. All the information available fits in this other frame, and, because

it provides a different meaning it makes possible different consequences.[10] Reframing is demonstrated in the clinical example of
Ms. S., a 28 year old woman pharmacist who came for counseling
for her alcoholism. She was self-identified as an alcoholic who
abused both alcohol and pills. She had suffered a divorce due to her
alcoholism. At the time she requested treatment, her job was at risk.

Ms. S. stated she wanted to do something about "how bad my
problem has gotten." She had attended Alcoholics Anonymous
(A.A.) for six months eighteen months earlier and had dropped out
because "I heard all that they had to say." For those six months Ms.
S. was abstinent of all mood altering chemicals. In the course of
treatment she did not follow through on any of the clinician's suggestions—suggestions which were already familiar to her through
her previous A.A. involvement. Ms. S. was holding firmly to her
request for treatment: "You've got to help me stop." No amount of
logical discussion of her situation and the supports available to her
motivated this woman to make a move towards abstinence.

When the logical approach yielded nothing, the worker responded by reframing Ms. S.'s situation as positive. This is particularly helpful if the client has tried all sorts of rational remedies prior
to this treatment. The intervention went like this: "Ms. S., you came
here very knowledgeable about your relationship to alcohol and
pills. You have researched options for yourself including A.A.
From the little you have told me it seems that your chemical use is
basically a good thing, a helpful thing. The use makes possible certain things in your life. For instance, you tell me that your parents
have sent you a check every other week since you lost your first job;
that your friend is available to you to come to your home and talk
with you all night when you call and tell her you are upset. I think
that it would be rash of you to plunge ahead into sobriety. There
would be much to loose." So often we become involved in convincing clients to do something. In the above therapeutic move Ms. S. is
encouraged through the reframe to consider a different way of looking at her situation.

In addition to providing a different meaning to an experience
which in turn makes different consequences possible, reframing
goes a long way towards freeing the clinician from a power struggle
with the client. This then diminishes resistance. The convincing
game of "stop using alcohol/chemicals because they are hurting
you" stabilizes client and clinician in a triangle with the third cor-

ner being the content of the argument. It was Buckminster Fuller who reminded us modern thinkers that the triangle is the sturdiest of geometric shapes. There is no triangle when the clinician reframes the status quo as positive and points out the disadvantages of change. This technique is particularly useful with resistant persons who, in order to resist the therapeutic injunction "don't change," must begin to change.[11]

In the case of Ms. S., the reframe was met initially with "what do you mean," and "that's crazy." Clinicians who begin to offer an absolutely different frame of a family or individual situation can expect such a reaction and can develop clinical responses that support the reframe. "I know that sounds crazy; it is such a different way to look at things," is an example.

After this first response of disbelief, Ms. S. began to discuss the dangers of drinking and pilling to her health. She began to develop reasons for abstinence that originated from her. This was qualitatively different from previous experiences of reasons for her to stop drinking and pilling which had originated from others.

The Al-Anon Program's detachment principle is a fine example of dismantling the triangle through reframe.[12] The Al-Anon family member, significant other, of an alcoholic learns a different definition of their experience. For example, the frame that a spouse is purposefully malicious in what s/he says is replaced with "it's the disease talking." The new frame that both alcoholic and significant others are ill from alcoholism provides all persons involved with new options.

Jane R.'s experience with the information she received from Al-Anon is illustrative of this. Prior to Al-Anon attendance Jane had been phsyically abused by her husband when he was drinking. When she was beaten by her husband during her seventh month of pregnancy, she was referred to an alcoholism clinic. Through the clinic involvement, she was introduced to Al-Anon. Jane was clear that she did not want to leave her marriage. She did, however, develop choices within it through the reframe that her husband was suffering from a disease. This new frame of her situation combined with the support that she received in Al-Anon made it possible for her to choose to leave her home with her two children whenever her husband returned intoxicated and also to choose not to meet him when he called from the train station and was drunk. Prior to Al-Anon involvement she would escort him home from the station when he called. Her husband refused treatment when it was offered to him. The most immediate and drastic change in family life was that Jane was no longer physically abused by her husband. Jane's husband remained unwilling to stop drinking until a severe medical problem developed two years later.

The reorganization of information into a new frame is effective given to families as well as individuals. The B.'s were in their forties and had been married twenty years when they requested treatment for Mrs. B's alcoholism. A clear picture of the marriage as a three generational enmeshed system emerged. The B's parents were involved in all major financial decisions as well as the day to day issues of management of the couple's home, children and Mrs. B.'s drinking. The clinician immediately moved to reframe the situation based on the history of repeated residential alcoholism treament. The reframe included: "Alcohol provides a mutual area for you to focus on in your relationship. It also provides a built in space adaptor to alternately be close to your parents and then have some time away from them. Alcohol is very helpful to you in managing your family life. Perhaps it is not wise to give it up." This was a totally new frame of the presence of alcohol in their lives. When they protested the reframe and planned a trip to their second home the clinician encouraged the husband to provide alcohol for his wife at their vacation site "in light of the importance of alcohol in your lives." After this move to underscore the reframe the couple withdrew from treatment. Their withdrawal was positively connoted in a letter the clinician sent supporting them on how carefully they had thought through the benefits of their present situation.[13] About six months later Mrs. B. called to tell the therapist that she had gone to another rehabilitation unit and that she was involved in A.A. She said that she and her husband were working on "putting our lives in order and I just wanted to tell you that we don't need alcohol in our family. That was a crazy idea you had."

Notice that in the above example and that of Ms. S., reframes are seemingly illogical. The decision to use reframing in both instances rested on the histories that had been given that previous logical approaches to alcoholism treatment had been unsuccessful. The reframing technique facilitated the process of client/system seriously considering the situation and what abstinence for the user and detachment for the significant other(s) meant in terms of losses. Reframing allows the client/system to use energy which had formerly been expended on resistance to facilitate change.[14]

TIME-LIMITED TREATMENT

The next case example illustrates the use of contracted sessions with reframing. Mr. G. was 33, married and employed in a retail clothing store. He initiated treatment because of pressure from his wife about his drinking. He readily agreed with the clinician's feedback to him on the information he had given about his situation: he had his drinking under control and his real problem was his wife's constant nagging.

Clinician and Mr. G. contracted for four sessions to discuss his relationship to alcohol and his problem of a nagging wife. He was open to doing a diagnostic interview for chemical dependency and responded to the assessment that he was chemically dependent with self-assurance that he could control his drinking.[15] He was pleased that his wife's nagging had diminished since he began to come to appointments. In the fourth session the therapeutic intervention was to end treatment with the instruction that Mr. G. continue to drink. This instruction was based on the assessment that Mr. G. had no intention of ceasing drinking. He requested additional sessions to keep his wife off his back. The clinician refused with a restatement of the instruction. He had successfully convinced his wife and subsequently an outside professional that his drinking was hurtful to him. The drinking he would continue to do was framed as necessary work in gathering more information about his alcohol use. Time-limited counseling with its built-in evaluation of treatment cuts down on the possibility of assisting an individual in his/her drinking through maintenance of the myth that s/he is doing something about the chemical abuse in counseling sessions.

Mr. G. entered residential treatment at his own initiative eight months later when he missed a Monday of work. The lost day's work did provide him with the information he needed to be open to abstinence. To summarize, Mr. G. was familiar with the litany of why he ought to stop drinking; if presented with that in therapy it would simply have been "more of the same."[16] In fact, reframing the active drinking as a way of gathering information and therefore a step in recovery, was something totally unexpected. The literature discusses the use of psychological shock to create confusion which leads to therapeutic shifts.[17] An additional piece of reframe used in this situation was to infrom Mr. G. that he was a winner. Since his task was to go out and learn more about his active use of alcohol he would be a winner if he stopped drinking on his own and he would be a winner if his drinking got out of hand thus clarifying the next step to take in recovery from alcoholism. The agreement in the first interview to meet four times for assessment provided a solid springboard to launch the client into the next phase of alcoholism treatment: learning more about the extent of his use of alcohol.

"GOING SLOW TO GET GOING"[18]

The next strategic posture to be discussed is encouraging a client/family to "go slow to get going." This stance assures the client that the clinician recognizes that change brings uncertainty and that therapy will proceed at a pace slow enough to help the client.[19]

An example of the technique of urging a person to "go slow to get going" is that of a 27 year old, single man who had been drinking since age 12. He described isolation from his family even though he lived at home. He also related his family's total acceptance of his drinking. The client had already identified for himself that he had a problem with alcohol. A near severe car accident and stomach pains motivated him to come for treatment. Mr. C. readily gave his drinking history. He had never had a social interaction since age 12 without alcohol. He had not had a sexual experience without alcohol and was unable to imagine his life without drinking. He knew intellectually that he needed to be dry to stay alive. He was clearly in a dilemma of "can't live with it and can't live without it."

Mr. C. was encouraged to go very slowly because there were so many unknowns involved in working towards his goal of abstinence. If he were to go to A.A., he was urged to go only to an open meeting to gather some facts that just might give him a glimpse of a possible future without alcohol. Certainly he would be expecting too much of himself to consider going to a meeting to become a member. Mr. C. did go to A.A. after a number of counseling sessions throughout which the worker maintained this tack. At the meeting he met a man sober for over a year and very involved in the A.A. Program who used to be a drinking buddy of his. By that time Mr. C. was ready to talk with this member. The use of "go slow" is shown in this example: the client should not consider joining A.A., it is too early. This does away with the possibility of client, clinician, content of "go to a meeting/won't go" triangulation. The stance of "go slow to get going" in this instance defines small moves the client can achieve.

USE OF METAPHOR

The final strategic tool to be discussed is the use of metaphors. "Metaphors are a way of talking about an experience."[20] A.A. and Al-Anon have both used this tool intuitively through the ritual of members sharing their stories. A story, after all, is a metaphor. Stories, tales, folk histories have been a part of every culture since the beginning of language, all sharing the ability to influence the listener in an indirect way.

Metaphor is an important tool in alcoholism treatment given the specific central nervous system damage that alcohol causes. The individual may be able to grasp the metaphorical representation of an issue more easily than the logical, direct discussion of that issue. All of us have such examples from our clinical practice: i.e., the person who is unable to talk directly about the immediate loss of a loved one, but rather focuses on the old loss of a pet, is doing important therapeutic mourning through metaphor.

There are two metaphors that I have used repeatedly in alcoholism treatment. In the first the chemical is likened to a lover who has turned on the person. The emotional experience of any love relationship gone sour includes the dilemma of how to end it, the pain of disappointed love, dashed dreams of the future, despondency at the thought of being without that loved one, etcetera. The therapy session would not look much like alcoholism counseling. Perhaps a whole session would be filled with the clinician telling stories of ended love affairs and new, more positive ones, replacing those affairs in time.

The second metaphor of climbing a steep mountain to represent recovery would have a series of metaphors within the metaphor. The pains in the leg muscles as the person, one step at a time, climbs up thousands of feet would be contrasted with the times of pain-free second winds. The metaphor would contain the experience of being too tired to eat lunch—that the lunch is packed but there is hardly any energy to open the pack and take it out to enjoy it. Perhaps, on the way, there are moments of unexpected beauty: a hummingbird above tree line, a beautiful view of a distant mountain range, a flower growing out of a crevice in a rock and so on. This metaphor parallels the difficulties of learning to live without alcohol both for individuals and families. The pain of a step up a steep hill is a metaphor for living through a difficult moment without alcohol; the lunch that the hiker is too tired to eat is a metaphor for the potential for intimate relationships; the top of the mountain is a metaphor for reaching goals (in this instance the goal of stable sobriety); the moments of unexpected beauty are metaphors for achievements in abstinence.

A wonderful story of the use of metaphor is in *The Teaching Tales of Milton H. Erickson.*[20] Erickson talked with an active alcoholic about the Desert Botanical Garden in Phoenix and a particular species of cactus. This cactus has the ability to survive for three years without water. The entire treatment consisted of one lengthy session in which Erickson told the man about the Garden and that amazing cactus with its ability to survive without water, a clear analogy to the patient's ability to survive without alcohol.

CONCLUSION

In conclusion, this paper has been developed to open new doors for clinicians involved in alcoholism treatment. It is appropriate to present an Erickson treatment story at this point for it was Milton Erickson teaching about resistance who stated "you can always walk around resistance . . . resistance belongs to the patient. You let him discover a way to use his resistance in a profitable way."[21] Clinicians taking the "walk around resistance" will find detailed route markers in the resources given throughout this work.

REFERENCE NOTES

1. See, for example, Deluca, J. (Ed.). *Fourth Special Report to the U.S. Congress on Alcohol and Health.* Rockville, Maryland: National Institute of Alcohol Abuse and Alcoholism, 1981.

2. Parsons, O. "Cognitive Dysfunction in Alcoholics and Social Drinkers." *Journal of Studies on Alcohol,* 1980, *41,* p.108.

3. Bennett, A. *Alcoholism and the Brain.* New York: Stratton Intercontinental Medical Book Corporation, 1977, p. 27.

4. Parsons, op. cit., pp.107-118.

5. Watzlawick, P., Weakland, J. & Fisch, R. *Change. Principles of Problem Formation and Problem Resolution.* New York: W.W. Norton, 1974.

6. Ibid., p.ix.

7. For a discussion of prescribing the symptom see Haley, J. *Uncommon Therapy. The Psychiatric Techniques of Milton H. Erickson.* New York: W.W. Norton, 1973; Raskin, D. & Klein, Z. Losing a symptom through keeping it. *Archives of General Psychiatry,* 1976, *33,* pp. 548-555; and, Watzlawick, Weakland & Fisch, op. cit.

8. Weakland, J. "Going slow to get going." Lecture given at the Don Jackson Memorial Conference, San Francisco, 1977.

9. Watzlawick, Weakland & Fisch, op. cit.

10. Ibid., pp. 92-109.

11. For a discussion of paradoxical intervention see Frankl, V. Paradoxical Intention, a Logotherapeutic Technique. *American Journal of Psychotherapy*, 1960, *14*, pp.520-535. For a bibliography on paradoxical methods see L'Abate, L. & Weeks, G. "A Bibliography of Paradoxical Methods in Psychotherapy of Family Systems." *Family Process*, 1978, *17*, pp. 95-98.

12. *What do you do about the alcoholic's drinking?* New York: Al-Anon Family Group Headquarters, 1966.

13. For a discussion of positive connotation see Palazzoli, M.S., Boscolo, L. Cecchin, G. & Prata, G. *Paradox and Counterparadox*. New York: Jason Aronson, 1978.

14. Saposnek, D. Aikido: "A Model for Brief Strategic Therapy." *Family Process*, 1980, *19*, pp. 227-238.

15. For a discussion of format for a diagnostic interview for alcoholism see Johnson, V. *I'll Quit Tomorrow*. New York: Harper & Row, 1973.

16. Watzlawick, Weakland & Fisch, op. cit., pp. 31-39.

17. For an example of psychological shock see Haley op. cit., pp. 164-166. For a discussion of same see Erickson, M. Rossi, E. & Rossi, S. *Hypnotic Realities*. New York: Irvington Publishers, 1976.

18. Weakland, op. cit.

19. Ibid.

20. Gordon, D. *Therapeutic Metaphors*. Cupertino, California: Meta Publications, 1978, p. 9.

21. Rosen, S. (Ed.). *My Voice Will Go With You. The Teaching Tales of Milton H. Erickson*. New York: W.W. Norton, 1982, pp. 80-81.

22. Milton H. Erickson, Seminar given in Phoenix, Arizona, June 1979.

Loss and Grief:
Major Dynamics in the Treatment
of Alcoholism

Marian Goldberg, A.C.S.W.

ABSTRACT. Loss and grief are major dynamics in the psychosocial treatment of alcoholism. Loss occurs in the pre-alcoholic, the alcoholic and the recovery periods. Doing grief work becomes a major focus of treatment to support sustained sobriety. Grieving the loss of alcohol itself is the first step in learning how to grieve other alcohol and non-alcohol related losses.

Loss is a universal experience; an experience that repeats itself throughout the stages of the life cycle. From the time of our birth until the time of our death, we are continually confronted with and tested by experiences of having lost, being without, being separated from and being deprived of objects once had and valued. While these experiences touch our vulnerability and leave us open to feelings of deep sadness, pain and grief, they also afford us the opportunity to struggle against and to come to terms with loss and pain. It is the involvement in the struggle, reflected by the grief work process that enhances our feelings of power, security and adaptability, and serves as a foundation for our maturation, growth and our ability to accept change.

Loss is a dominant theme in the dynamics and psychosocial treatment of alcoholism. Psychosocial histories of a large number of alcoholics tell of either reactive or incremental drinking after loss. Specific to the process of addiction and the progression of the disease of alcoholism are a variety of significant losses. Loss is intrinsic to the process of recovery when the bottle, as well as the old maladaptive psychosocial mechanisms, must be given up and replaced by healthier responses to life's situations.

Prepared for presentation at the NASW 12th Annual All-Day Alcoholism Institute held at Fordham University, New York City, May 20, 1980.

37

In this paper, I will examine the general subject of loss, and in particular, loss in relation to the alcoholic and the disease of alcoholism. In discussion the process of restitution from loss, through the successful completion of grief work and the alcoholic's difficulties with this process will be outlined. Thereafter, implications for alcoholism treatment of the individual and groups will be elaborated upon.

LOSS AND THE GRIEF WORK PROCESS

In our society, the most recognized loss is death. However, during our growth and development, we experience other losses which are more subtle. Because of the nature of these losses, their true identification, value and impact, as loss, is often overlooked. David Peretz has clearly outlined four forms of loss: loss of a significant loved or valued person which can occur through death, illness, divorce, or separation; loss of some aspect of self which can occur with changes in ideas and feelings about the self, or with loss of health, body function, social roles or self definition; loss of external objects, such as possessions, home or homeland; and developmental loss which occurs in the process of human growth and development.[1] Since it is the individual who endows loss with personal and symbolic meaning, it is only he who can differentiate between major and minor losses and their impact. Something perceived as a major loss by one person may not be seen as loss at all by another. In addition, since all losses and separations merge in the unconscious, the impact of loss, if unresolved, can be cumulative.

Grief and mourning are the normal reactions to loss. In order to accept and integrate loss, one must be able to mourn, that is to say, allow oneself to react to the loss of the object and thereafter to readjust to an external environment in which the object no longer exists in reality.[2] Our experiences with mourning early losses will generally determine the way we react to and deal with future losses. In the grief work process we first confront the shock that results from the sudden upset of the ego equilibrium when we become aware that the object no longer exists.[3] This shock brings an awareness that precipitates the second stage of the mourning process which is the grief reaction itself. With the grief reaction we experience intense psychic and physical pain as a result of the separation, and the beginning of ego-object decathexis with the recognition of the loss.[3] In experiencing grief and throughout the grief process, feelings of anxiety, tension, pain, confusion, bewilderment, emptiness, yearning for the lost object, loneliness, guilt, anger, disappointment, depression, irritability and helplessness all come to the fore. By experiencing these feelings we develop the foundation to advance to the third and chronic stage of grief in which we merge the internal experience of loss with reality, and become once more free to see and form new attachments.[2] What becomes clear is that the *key* to the ability to deal effectively with loss, is the ability to do grief work. That is to say, to have an ego structure that will allow oneself to feel the pain of loss and to experience the intensity of feelings that arise throughout the process. Without this ability pathological reactions to unresolved grief develop. Alcoholism is a well documented pathological reaction to unresolved grief.

LOSS, GRIEF AND ALCOHOLISM

The author is not naive enough to assert that unresolved grief is the cause of alcoholism. However, it is known that alcoholics have difficulty in dealing with intense feelings, including those related to loss, and that the drug alcohol is often used to assuage the anxiety brought on by them. Therefore, it is not surprising that the ability or lack of ability to come to terms with loss and grief, and thus transcend them, has to be a major factor in the dynamics and treatment of alcoholism. The importance of recognizing this factor is essential when we consider the multitude of losses that occur through excessive drinking and during the process of recovery from alcoholism. Kellerman lists some of the losses resulting from drinking behavior: the loss of the ability to drink in keeping with the social norm; the loss of memory of drinking experiences; the loss of ability to choose not to drink and to stick to that choice; the loss of ability to maintain responsible social behavior when drinking; the loss of the ability to regain sobriety once intoxicated.[3] Another common and substantial loss that is drink related is loss of control of bodily function. Once the alcoholic is alcohol free, he is confronted by losses which are the consequences of his drinking behavior as well as by losses associated with recovery. These losses include: the loss of alcohol with abstinence; the loss of employment, financial status and educational opportunity; the loss of relationships with significant others; the loss of physical health, self-esteem, self-respect, and self confidence;

the loss of the pre-alcoholic self-concept; the loss of the self-image of the drunk; and the loss of unrealized expectations.[4]

A major portion of the task of psychosocial treatment in alcoholism is working to enable the alcoholic to deal with grief and feelings associated with loss. Through this work, the alcoholic comes to tolerate anxiety and change and moves out of his social isolation; he exchanges feelings of self-pity and self-hate for feelings of self-love and lessens his chance of relapse.

Anyone doing psychosocial treatment with alcoholics is aware of the need for caution in confronting anxiety-producing issues. The fear is that the anxiety will be too much for the alcoholic to handle and thus he will resort to the old familiar "helper," alcohol. This may result in avoidance of addressing grief work issues by helping professionals. The author has found that if the alcoholic can have the experience of grieving one loss, to be specific, the loss of alcohol, the ego structure is strengthened. This then enables the alcoholic to tolerate anxiety experienced from other losses. Therefore, the question becomes, not whether to start the grief work process, but when to start and what to focus on.

GRIEF WORK AND ALCOHOLISM

We know that when the alcoholic first becomes sober, he is preoccupied with thoughts of alcohol. He has painful repetitious recollections of drinking and drinking experiences, and he tries to make sense out of having to give up alcohol. These mental processes are component parts of the grief work process.[5] Considering that the alcoholic has already begun the process, the most appropriate focus for the process of grief work is alcohol itself.

The facilitating process begins in the initial phase of the alcoholism treatment with the worker's taking the first drinking history. With achievement of sobriety and movement towards the development and availability of adaptive tools that foster abstinence, one can consider moving on if the patient is ready, to grieve other alcohol related losses and those losses from the pre-alcoholic period. This movement becomes part of the "work of recovery" in the middle phase of alcoholism treatment.[4] Of course, if an alcoholic brings material regarding a current loss into the treatment setting, no matter what the timing, it must be addressed. The worker will need to use judgement regarding how much gets opened up around the loss to keep the resultant anxiety at a manageable level.

The importance of grieving the loss of alcohol first is validated by the literature on pathological grief. Pathological grief reactions occur most frequently when the relationship with the lost object is not anticipated, where the relationship had been highly ambivalent and stormy, where the loss was caused by self-destruction, where the lost object evokes oppressive feelings of guilt and where the real world left behind changes without the lost object.[6] This seems an accurate description of the relationship between alcohol and the alcoholic: immature, dependant, ambivalent, stormy, self-destructive, guilty and changing.

The major goal of alcoholism treament is sobriety. Only when sobriety is achieved can we address maladaptation in other psychosocial areas. There is no question that grief work focused on the loss of alcohol must be a priority in therapy in order for the alcoholic to have a better chance to sustain sobriety.

IMPLICATIONS FOR TREATMENT

The bereavement literature also offers some direction on how to proceed with grief work in alcoholism treatment. Eric Lindemann describes successful grief work as requiring the completion of the following tasks: the bereaved must separate himself or herself from the deceased by breaking the bond that holds them together; he must readjust to the environment from which the deceased is missing; he must form new relationships.[7] Similar steps are required for successful maintenance of sobriety. The alcoholic must separate himself physically and emotionally from alcohol. He must readjust to living without alcohol by altering his thinking attitudes and behavior. He must form new relationships within his environment which are appropriate for his chemically free state. The worker's task is to enhance and facilitate the grieving process, to enable the achievement of successful grief work, and therefore strengthen sobriety. Towards this end, the author believes that Beverly Raphael's model for the management of pathological grief[8] can be adapted to alcoholism treatment. The material that follows will demonstrate how this can be done.

When treatment begins, the therapist establishes a contract with the individual or the group which outlines specifically the goals and tasks of the therapy. In forming the contract the worker should alert patients that grief work will be part of their work of recovery focused on the consequences of living with or without alcohol. The worker should also educate the patients about the grief work process and its relation to their achieving and maintaining sobriety.

As part of the ongoing therapeutic work which needs to be ego supportive and reassuring, a comprehensive review of the patient's drinking history should be taken to provide an opening to gather material that will be utilized throughout the course of treatment. In taking the history there will be opportunities for grief work: in exploring the way in which the loss took place (e.g., alcohol given up); in exploring memories of the lost object (e.g., drinking, drinking experiences and drinking behavior); in exploring memories of the preexisting relationship (e.g., the meaning and function of alcohol during the progression of the disease); and in exploring the affect of the bereavement (e.g., feelings of anxiety, tension, emotional and physical pain, confusion, bewilderment, emptiness, yearning for alcohol, loneliness, guilt, anger, disappointment, depression, irritability and helplessness as they relate to the progression of the disease of alcoholism and the process of recovery). Clarification of details will allow for ventilation and may also reveal elements of denial. Bringing denial to consciousness and confronting its elements is an extremely important part of alcoholism treatment. It is patients' denial of the disease, its seriousness, its impact as well as their denial of the difficulty in staying sober that often leads to their return to alcohol use. It is important to note that the material taken as part of the history will provide information on other alcohol and non-alcohol related losses that may need to be addressed in the same manner during the course of treatment.

Throughout treatment, anxieties related to being without the lost object (i.e., alcohol) should be explored. The viewing of photographs or other objects related to the loss may help. At the St. Luke's Hospital Comprehensive Alcoholism Treatment Program some rich grief work took place in groups to which the therapist brought a prop of a large plastic liquor bottle to stimulate discussion. The prop served as a visualization facilitating the recognition of the patients' feelings about the lost object, alcohol. This evoking of alcohol related memories and their associated feelings enabled the grief work process to proceed. Patients confronted their perceptions of the drinking experience more realistically and were thus able to weigh the pros and cons as compared to sober living. Through this process, their commitment to sustained abstinence was reinforced. As repetition of material presented and discussed is necessary for the bereaved to master loss,⁹ repetition is also necessary for the alcoholic to help compensate for the pharmacological effects of alcoholism on the central nervous system (i.e., cognitive dysfuntion, poor memory, etc.), and to break through and combat denial. Those doing alcoholism treatment will do well to review material pertaining to the loss of alcohol and alcohol related losses in a wide variety of groups. Educational groups, motivational groups, sobriety groups, "rap" groups, support groups, film groups, and more intensive psychotherapeutic groups for patients with more stabilized sobriety can all include grief work as part of their work on recovery. Bellwood has also described the use and success of psychodrama and art therapy as vehicles for doing grief work in alcoholism treatment.[10]

In continuing her discussion of the management of pathological grief, Beverly Raphael further outlines treatment techniques which can be effective in grieving the loss of alcohol. She suggests: that the appropriateness and normalcy of sadness, sense of loss or other affect such as guilt, anger, shame or dependency should be communicated by the therapist; that the patient should be encouraged to express these feelings; that the origins of specific angers and guilts should be explored; and that the therapist needs to acknowledge bad feelings and the pain of grief.[x] If the therapist can teach the alcoholics to identify and label their emotional states, they can learn and use more adequate emotional responses. Having an expanded repertoire of behaviors to relieve painful feeling states, they need not be as prone to resort to alcohol to do so. Interpretation of defenses contributing to inhibition of grief may be provided.[x] In alcoholism treatment, such defenses are often heard as the patient stating that, "everything is fine," despite the upheaval existing from past drinking and current engagement in the struggle for sobriety. Patients' experience that "everything is fine" in new recovery should be validated as common and natural since compared to the state of affairs while drinking things are, in fact, markedly improved. However, patients also need to be advised of the traps into which they can fall if they perceive their recovery from that point alone. The worker should not be surprised to hear the patients idealize the lost object, alcohol, and should not get frightened by this material or try to stop its flow. Instead, the therapist should allow this material and counter-balance it by reaching for the realities of the negative side of the patients' experience with drinking. This is a technique for working through the patients' ambivalence towards giving up alcohol and other lost objects.

Lastly, one cannot over-emphasize the importance of promoting an appropriate social support network for the successful resolution of grief.[8] Such a network serves to fill the void created by the loss and to support the bereaved through the period of grief to resolution. In the St. Luke's Program, which operates to a great degree as a day center, the group process facilitates and enhances the development of the ability to grieve through mutual support and identification. For over forty years, Alcoholic Anonymous has proven the need for and success of a sober social support system.

The program of recovery of Alcoholics Anonymous is one of the most important networks for the alcoholic. This program facilitates the alcoholic in working through to resolution the loss of alcohol and other alcohol and non-alcohol related losses. A.A. provides the alcoholic with a support system to fill the void of the loss; it provides role models in those who have let go of alcohol and completed their grief work; it also provides the opportunity to establish new social roles to replace those lost in drinking and in recovery. It provides a new self-concept of "the alcoholic" in place of the old self-concept as "the drunk." Of importance are the Twelve Steps of Recovery in the A.A. program.[11] The "Steps" offer the option of replacing the loss of the bottle with the gain of a Higher Power. This, in turn, fosters the process of "letting go." The fourth step inventory is a vehicle for reviewing the past, for "letting go" of it and for finding ways to make peace with angers, guilts, and resentments. In the Qualification, the alcoholic talks about where he is, where he has been, how he is recovering and things he hopes can be part of his continued recovery. The Qualification provides an opportunity for exploration and ventilation about the past. It carries the alcoholic through the process of restitution through his sharing the gain of recovery achieved by accepting the loss of the bottle. The Promises of the Program[12] provide hope that if one gives up the bottle, a new and enriched life will replace it.

We cannot end a paper on grief work and alcoholism without making note of the therapist. In the process of doing this work, the therapist's own losses and their concomitant feelings will be engaged. Thus, it is important that the therapist come to terms with his own psychodynamics about loss and that he continues to develop and maintain an awareness of his own feelings and conflicts about loss. Such understanding may require the therapist's commitment to take steps to work through his own unfinished business about losses in his own life.

REFERENCES

1. Peretz D: *Development, Object-Relationships, and Loss in Loss and Grief: Psychological Management in Medical Practice*. Edited by Schoenberg B, Carr A C, Peretz D, et al. New York, Columbia University Press, 1970

2. Pollack G H: "Mourning and Adaption." *The International Journal of Psychoanalysis* 42: 341-361, 1961

3. Kellermann C M: *Grief: A Basic Reaction to Alcoholism*. Center City, Minnesota, Hazelden, 1977

4. Goldberg M: The "Work of Recovery" in the Middle Phase of Alcoholism Treatment: A Psychosocial Task Oriented Framework in *Social Work Treatment of Alcohol Problems*. Vol. 5 in RUCAS-NIAAA Treatment Series. Edited by Cook D, Fewell C, Riolo J. New Brunswick, New Jersey, Rutgers Center of Alcohol Studies, 1983

5. Parkes C M: *Bereavement: Studies of Grief in Adult Life*. New York, International University Press, 1972

6. Volkan V D: *The Recognition and Prevention of Pathological Grief*. Virginia Medical Monthly 99: 535-540, 1972

7. Lindermann, E: *Symptomatology and Management of Acute Grief in Crisis Intervention: Selected Readings*. Edited by Parad H. New York, Family Service Association of America, 1965

8. Raphael B: *The Management of Pathological Grief*. Australian and New Zealand Journal of Psychiatry 9: 173-180, 1975

9. Simos B G: "Grief Therapy to Facilitate Healthy Restitution:" *Social Casework* 58: 337-342, 1977

10. Bellwood L R: "Grief Work in Alcoholism Treatment." *Alcohol Health and Research World* Spring: 8-11, 1975

11. Alcoholics Anonymous: *Twelve Steps and Twelve Traditions*. New York, Alcoholics Anonymous World Services, Inc, 1952

12. Alcoholics Anonymous: *Alcoholics Anonymous*. 2nd ed. New York, Alcoholics Anonymous World Services, Inc, 1955

The Integration of Sexuality Into Alcoholism Treatment

Christine Huff Fewell, A.C.S.W.

ABSTRACT. Sexuality is usually ignored in alcoholism treatment programs, but it is often an issue about which patients are secretly very concerned. While timing of more detailed discussion about sexual issues should often be postponed until sobriety is well established, there are diagnostic issues which need to be addressed. Information about the role sexual conflicts may have played in the alcoholism are important to determine. Information about sexuality needs to be given to patients in alcoholism treatment programs. A sample educational lecture based on a review of the literature on alcoholism and sexuality is given.

Sexual counselling for people with alcohol problems is a relatively new area of consideration in the alcoholism literature and the field, which is not surprising when we think that only some ten years ago did programs to help people with alcoholism become widely established. Increasingly, however, practitioners are turning their attention to both what role sexuality may play in alcoholic relationships and to what kind of counselling about sexuality may be helpful to alcoholic people, and their partners. This paper will briefly review relevant studies on the effects of alcohol consumption and abuse on sexual functioning and will highlight some of the issues in treatment. Clinical examples of some of the different roles played by alcohol in sexual functioning will be discussed. The educational role these observations and studies might have for alcoholic patients and their partners will be incorporated into the outline of an educational lecture which might be given to patients or significant others in an alcoholism treatment facility.

REVIEW OF THE LITERATURE

Early experimental studies dealt with the effects of alcohol on the sexual response of animals. In their review of these studies Carpenter and Armenti[1] concluded that these experiments do not constitute a sufficient base for reaching conclusions concerning the relation between alcohol and human sexual behavior.

Recent studies on humans by Rubin and Henson[2] show that alcohol has a depressant effect on sexual responsiveness according to the dosage consumed. In lower doses drinking alcohol affects men by delaying ejaculation. Speed of arousal and degree of erection are not affected. The men studied (who were all college-age volunteers) reported their belief that alcohol enhanced their sexual functioning and continued to believe that after the experiment proved to the contrary. The conclusion of the study was that men and women may well prefer or seek the effects of small amounts of alcohol on their sexual functioning. In fact, men who suffer from premature ejaculation may have possibly even sought out alcohol for its delaying effect on ejaculation without realizing it.

Two other studies (by Farkas and Rosen[3] on men and Wilson and Lawson[4] on women) measured genital response to erotic visual stimulation at varying doses of alcohol and found that increasing intoxication in both women and men resulted in progressively reduced sexual arousal.

Another major popular belief is that alcohol reduces inhibitions. There is some evidence to support the belief that alcoholics perceive alcohol as being sexually facilitating or releasing them from inhibitions. Beckman[5] questioned 477 people including 120 women alcoholics, 120 male alcoholics, 119 non-alcoholic person control group, and 118 non-alcoholic women in treatment for other emotional problems. One conclusion of this study was that greater desire for, enjoyment of and reported frequency of sexual relations after drinking are more characteristic of alcoholism than other types of psychopathology in women. In this study a significant proportion of women alcoholics reported fairly low sexual satisfaction and believed that alcohol improved their sexual enjoyment and decreased their inhibitions.

These women alcoholics studied perceived these as positive effects of alcohol. These findings have an important consequence for treatment, says Beckman; " . . . if beliefs concerning the effects of drinking on sexuality do promote drinking among women, it would appear that treatment programs should try to disrupt, perhaps through educational programs, the cognitive link between alcohol and improved sexual functioning. Also, when treating women alcoholics, therapists can promote methods other than drinking for increasing sexual enjoyment."[6]

Whalley[7] studied 50 alcoholic men who were hospitalized in Scotland and compared them to a control group of 50 men picked at random from a labor union who were carefully matched for age and economic class. He found striking similarities among them. However, the alcoholics expressed greater dissatisfaction with their sex lives. This appeared to have originated from a combination of their greater preferred frequency of sexual intercourse, reduced opportunities and their more frequent erectile impotence.

McClelland[8] and his associates at Harvard have studied alcohol in terms of the psychological effects of drinking on men and the psychological states which motivate men to drink. Small to moderate amounts of alcohol were found to increase thoughts of social power or power for the good of others or a cause. Larger amounts of alcohol increased thoughts of personal power, or power in the interest of self-aggrandisement, without regard for others. McClelland concluded that men drink primarily to feel stronger. Those for whom personalized power is a particular concern drink more heavily.

Women, however, were found to be influenced by alcohol in a different way than men. Wilsnack[9,10] studied women's attitudes about their sex roles before and after drinking and the effects of drinking on their fantasies. She found that power imagery was decreased and dependency themes were not affected. Instead drinking enhanced feelings of traditional femininity or womanliness. The studies suggest that women may drink because of sex role conflict between their perceptions of what they should be, what they want to be, and what is expected of them. Wilsnack concluded that "a woman troubled in this way may drink in part to restore her feelings of feminine adequacy and womanliness."

In summarizing the findings in the literature regarding the effects of alcohol on sexual functioning we can see that alcohol has been found to be used by alcoholic women to decrease inhibitions about sexual functioning. Alcohol is seen by some men as facilitating sexual functioning and in fact when used in moderate amounts it delays ejaculation which is seen as desirable by both men and women. However, in larger amounts it retards or makes impossible sexual functioning in both men and women. Prolonged alcohol abuse may cause impotence in men long after sobriety due to damage to the neurologic reflex arc.[11]

Increasing tolerance to alcohol also means that more and more alcohol is needed to effect fewer and fewer sexual results. Just as in other aspects of alcoholism that are so familiar to us, cause and effect become confused. People may have begun drinking to deal with sexual and aggressive conflicts (as postulated by Sharoff).[12] However, once excessive drinking leads to impotence in men, panic sets in[13] bringing secondary impotence and other psychological problems which cause the man to take more and more alcohol to deal with fears of lack of masculinity. The same may well be true of women when they don't lubricate and drink to feel more sexy or womanly. Since the lack of ability to perform in alcoholics does not always take away the desire for sex, this creates further conflicts.[14]

It is interesting to note that even though it was not objectively true, the men studied by Rubin and Henson felt that their sexual performance was improving as they drank more and were less able to perform. The women studied by Wilsnack felt that drinking made them feel less inhibited and more sexy. It would seem that the euphoric recall as described by Vernon Johnson[15] is responsible for this phenomenon.

INTERVENTION IN DIFFERENT STATES OF TREATMENT: DIAGNOSTIC ISSUES

In alcoholic marriages or sexual relationships involving an alcoholic sex is almost always a problem because of: (1) the physiological effects of alcohol, and (2) because of the anger that has built up.

THE IMPORTANCE OF HISTORY TAKING

Deciding when to introduce discussion about sexual material is one of the initial considerations. The overriding issue to be dealt with first in all alcoholism treatment is sobriety. It may be six months to a year before the individual is secure enough in sobriety to tackle any detailed material about sexual functioning. However, in order to help establish sobriety it may be diagnostically important to determine the role sexual conflicts played in the alcoholism and conversely, the role that alcoholism played in the sexual conflicts of that individual. Continued sobriety may well depend on altering the relationship between sexual conflicts and alcohol. The study by Beckman pointed out that women alcoholics said they drank in order to reduce inhibitions and feel more comfortable in sexual functioning. When these women give up drinking, new ways of dealing with these conflicts need to be found. Just as the process of taking a detailed drinking history makes the patient focus attention and allows him or her to tie together cause and effect in a new relationship, so pointing out the role played by alcohol in sexual functioning can be of similar benefit.

For example, in dealing with a couple's relationship, it would be helpful to know how they felt about their sexual functioning. Were they happy with it? Did they have intercourse only when drinking? Was alcohol used to deal with anxiety about intimacy? Who initiated the sexual contact? Was it only the alcoholic person when drinking? Or, on the other hand, was alcohol used to avoid sexual contact either because the non-alcoholic person was repulsed by the alcoholic person when he/she was drunk or because he/she was using refusal of sex as a way of trying to control the other's drinking?

EVALUATING THE KIND OF SEXUAL CONTENT

Diagnostically, another point to keep in mind in exploring a history of sexual functioning is that when a couple reports that they are not having sexual intercourse, this does not mean that there is no sexual content to their relationship. Many couples share a very intimate relationship necessitated by the caretaking required by alcoholics. Frequently alcoholics in the late stages of alcoholism lose control of bowel and bladder functioning and partners are witnesses or are in the position of cleaning up after the alcoholic. Certainly there is intimacy and there is also sexual pleasure to be had from the voyeuristic excitation inherent in witnessing such events.[16] And such a sexual component (albeit a regressed one) to a caretaking relationship may make it harder to give up when the alcoholic person gets sober, especially since there may be fears about sexual adequacy on both partners' parts after a long period of inactivity. The couple with this kind of relationship will need to be approached cautiously in dealing with the issue of their sexual relationship. The intimacy they do have should not be overlooked or minimized. If the need this intimacy may have served for both parties is recognized by the therapist, the couple can be helped to gradually channel this need into other more positive interactions.

SEXUAL ACTING OUT

Sexual acting out while drinking is another area to examine diagnostically. Because of their conflicts and inhibitions, many homosexuals as well as heterosexuals are unable to participate in any sexual activity unless drinking. Sometimes a person who has only functioned heterosexually may, during the period of alcoholic drinking, become involved in homosexual relationships due to regressed ego functioning as a whole. Other men and women become involved in heterosexual relationships while drunk as a defense against their underlying and unacceptable wish to have a homosexual relationship.

In many instances the need for closeness and holding, rather than a desire for sex, may have been the primary motivation for drunken encounters. Revenge fantasies against men or women may have been a motivating force for others. The specific facts about each individual's case and the meaning it has for him or her must be determined.

CONFLICTS WITH SEXUAL INTIMACY

Another behavior pattern which often emerges relates to the recurrent remorse experienced by many alcoholics. This remorse after drinking causes the alcoholic to be extremely attentive and seductive to his/her partner when sober, giving him/her the feeling of being very desirable. This aspect of the drinking/sober pattern may not be conscious to the people involved and the non-alcoholic partner may not want to lose the intimacy and attention which grows from this alternating remorse. Identifying these patterns would be helpful to the continued sobriety of the alcoholic.

The regulation of sexual intimacy conflicts through an alternating drinking/sober pattern, can be illustrated by Mary and Phil MacDonald, a couple seen in treatment together. Mary claimed that she always knew when Phil was drinking again because he would stay away from home for longer periods, only returning after Mary was asleep. He thus avoided the anger that she expressed towards him. When the drinking finally reached a point that he had to stop drinking in order to keep working, Mary would be able to express all her anger and Phil would be very remorseful. When sober, Phil was sexually passive, although attentive and helpful with the house and their four young children. During sober periods Mary would initiate sexual contact.

The reason for this pattern can be traced to Mary and Phil's families of origin. Mary came from a family with a brutal, chronic alcoholic father who had beaten her mother and had intercourse with her when he was drunk. Mary's father was also physically abusive to her on a number of occasions. Mary found a husband on whom she projected her conflicted feelings about the expression of sexuality. On the one hand, when he was drinking and expressing a lack of sexual inhibition, she was repulsed by him. When he was sober and holding back, she felt safe in initiating sexual contact. But he did not feel able to give freely then, so that again she was safe from being overwhelmed by sexual feelings and was not a helpless victim, but the aggressor. Phil came from a family where the father and mother expressed no sexual feelings openly and his father was extremely rigid and unable to be pleased. He always criticized Phil for not doing better in school although he was a good student. He felt he could not win father's love and admiration. Phil needed the alcohol in order to release inhibitions about sexuality and about his shaky feeling of masculine identity.

On the one hand, Mary seemed to want Phil to be sober very much. She attended Al-Anon and therapy. Mary's change in behavior towards Phil had caused him to seek treatment in a rehabilitation program. She had begun to function much more independently. She had convinced her mother to take a stand with her father, resulting in his gaining two months of sobriety for the first time in many years. However, the conflicts surfaced and could be seen in the incidents which follow.

Mary and Phil went to an engagement party in her sister's office with all of their old friends and they came directly from there to the session. Mary was high after having two drinks. While acting indulgently amused by his wife's good spirits, Phil began to talk about how he was not an alcoholic. In the following session, Mary expressed her anger and apprehension about Phil's saying that he was not an alcoholic, because although he was not drinking, this meant he might start at any minute. The next session was a stormy one. Mary and Phil had had a real confrontation at the wedding. Mary had gotten drunk and smoked pot for the first time in her life with the other members of the bridal party. She became very high and was quite frightened by it and out of control of herself. At the same time Phil was in the main reception room, not drinking and watching the four children. He began to get reports about how seductive and gay his wife was acting with the other men. He felt enraged and emasculated. It was only a few weeks before he began drinking again. As Mary reported to me, she saw the pornographic magazines and then she knew. By drinking and acting seductively uninhibited towards other men in public she had teased, enraged and humiliated Phil. When *he* acted uninhibited, she was not about to tolerate it. Both of them had difficulty releasing or tolerating their sexual feelings without the use of alcohol. At the same time the rather calm equilibrium which they had worked out over the eight months of sobriety did not hold enough release for them. As much pain as the other way of life brought for them, it seems that Mary missed the excitement of the drinking and that Phil's shaky masculine identity needed the alcohol in order to allow his fantasies to be expressed. Mary really precipitated the drinking bout by her husband in unconsciously behaving in a way which would increase his sense of masculine inferiority and increase his desire to drink.

POWER STRUGGLES IN THE SEXUAL ARENA

Another example of sexual interaction and its relationship to alcohol is shown by the Browns. Bill and Celia Brown had been living together for 12 years although they were not married. They came for joint counselling with their sexual problems after Bill had been sober for six months. This couple, now in their fifties, had had a very active sex life at the beginning of their relationship until Bill's drinking had progressed to around-the-clock drinking. Celia worked as a nurse's aide to support them and they began living in separate bedrooms. She performed many caring functions for him such as cooking, feeding and cleaning him. He finally went into a detoxification program and then spent six months going to a day hospital where he worked on his overwhelming feelings of shyness and inadequacy, and made great progress in being able to relate to other people.

As soon as he was sober, Celia began making demands for sexual intercourse which he could not satisfy because he was impotent (although he had erections during sleep). The couple was involved in an enormous power struggle as he looked for things to criticize her for in retaliation, such as her being overweight and thus unattractive to him. Initially, the couple was asked to put aside the idea of intercourse while an effort was made to sort out the feelings they were having. The result was that Celia's jealousy of Bill's freedom now that he was sober, and her fear that she would lose him to another woman, was revealed. The feelings of inadequacy which Celia was having needed to be worked on in some separate sessions. It then became possible for the couple to resume a sexual relationship as they were able to express their true feelings for each other without the pressures of the hidden agendas they each carried.

THE INFLUENCE OF PARENTAL ALCOHOLISM ON SEXUALITY

Another issue often encountered in the sexual problems of alcoholics relates to the fact that many alcoholic patients had parents who were alcoholics and who exhibited otherwise disturbed behavior. As children they were influenced in their view of sexuality by experiencing violent, overstimulating or seductive behavior by parents. There is a need in many cases to go back over the childhood history to help the patient understand the parents' behavior.[17] An aspect of this to be remembered is the sexual implications of the parents' behavior on the sexual development of the child. Since alcohol does release inhibitions, (although sexual functioning may be impaired), people who are drunk are often very seductive or give seductive innuendos to the most innocuous things they say without any awareness of this. To a child, however, it is confusing and overstimulating to be exposed to a parent who is acting this way.

For example, an alcoholic woman named Betty, had an alcoholic father who used to come home from the bar at 3 A.M. and line all the children up in the living room and make them watch while he hit the mother. The mother would not allow the children to interfere, which she might have believed was for their protection. On the other hand, by tolerating this behavior, she gave her children the message, "This is the way we have our fun." Betty married a very handsome, successful, narcissistic man who had many affairs with other women which she denied for a long time. Meanwhile her own alcoholism progressed to the point that she eventually lost her children. She incorporated the masochism and the absolute inability to have wishes or be entitled to any opinion. After her divorce from her husband and an interval of eight years during which she was mostly sober and had no sexual relationships, she began drinking again when she met a man and began having sex with him. Before intercourse she would go into the bathroom and drink a bottle of vodka in order to feel able to participate in sex. For her, being drunk was an essential ingredient of sex, through the identification with her father. But like mother she had also to be a masochistic victim who was mistreated.

TREATMENT ISSUES

Possibly the first intervention in dealing with the sexual relationship of an alcoholic person or an alcoholic couple may be to advise them to wait to deal with sexual issues until they are comfortable in sobriety. They need to be reassured that in most cases sexual functioning and sexual desire return to normal after a period of abstinence, but that it often takes months or even a year or more, for this to happen. They must be helped not to add anxiety about sexual issues to the many anxieties they will be facing in early sobriety. While having sexual intercourse as a goal may be postponed, the couple can be helped to explore other forms of sexual intimacy such as cuddling, touching, kissing, fondling and masturbating. Masturbation in lieu of seeking a partner at an early stage of sobriety might be explored. It is often said that when people begin drinking early in adolescence they arrest the trial and error learning of courtship in relationships. When they become sober years later, they are at a loss how to proceed. Just as the emotional side of the relationship building has suffered, so too has the physical counterpart of expressing feelings through cuddling and touching.

We are arriving at a point where there is acceptance of the idea that the family system will need time and possibly help to readjust to a sober member. We recognize that communication will be in need of repair, but communication on the sexual level is not addressed in the majority of treatment programs. While treatment of sexual dysfunction usually needs to be postponed until sobriety is well established, information about sexual functioning needs to be gotten from the patient and given to the patient towards the beginning of the treatment. First, it is very important to have information about sexual functioning at the beginning of treatment to see to what extent the alcoholic person may be drinking in order to deal with sexual conflicts.

This does *not* mean that discussion of the conflicts and alleviation of the guilt which often surrounds them can by themselves assist the person in remaining sober.

The ways that alcohol has interfered with sexual functioning may also be used as a powerful motivating tool in breaking down denial,[18] since the treating person will be looking for ways to impress upon the patient the effect that alcohol has had upon all areas of functioning—physical and social.

INTEGRATING DISCUSSION OF SEXUAL FUNCTIONING INTO ALCOHOLISM EDUCATION

Most alcoholism treatment programs have a series of educational lectures covering such topics as recognition of alcoholic symptoms, the kind of thinking used by alcoholics such as denial, rationalization and projection, what to expect from recovery, how to deal with slips, relating to AA, etc. Given the information gleaned from the studies about the influence of alcohol on sexual functioning and relating this to clinical experience, I would like to propose the following sample educational lecture for alcoholic people and/or their partners which summarizes the major points made above.

"Alcohol and Your Sex Life: How Do They Interrelate?"

You may wonder why we are dealing with the subject of sex in this lecture when you are very worried about how to avoid taking the next drink. The fact is that many people drink to help them deal with feelings about sex. So we feel that it may be important in helping you get sober to talk a little about you and sex and alcohol and how they interrelate.

Here are some of the common feelings people have about sex:

1) Guilt and shame
2) Anger
3) Jealousy
4) Fear

Let's see what these feelings relate to.

1) Guilt and shame. Many alcoholics end up behaving sexually in ways they wouldn't have if not drinking. Sometimes people end up having one night stands with people they meet in bars. Perhaps they wake up the next morning in a blackout, not remembering having met the person with whom they are in bed. Often they feel terrible about themselves, but the same thing keeps happening over and over again. There is no control over the alcohol and no control over the behavior once the drinking begins.

Other men and women have homosexual relationships when they are drinking which they wouldn't allow themselves otherwise. Does this mean they are homosexuals? Perhaps and perhaps not. If there is conflict, if it bothers you, it's something to work out and discuss in the counselling sessions to get help with at the right time.

2) Anger. Many alcoholics' relationships are full of anger and sex has become the battlefield for this anger. It may be blamed for all sorts of problems. Often people say, "I drink because my wife won't have sex with me." "I go out to bars and pick up men because my husband will not make love to me." "Which came first?," is the question. Often spouses refuse to have sex with a partner who is drunk (and this is no wonder). If a couple is fighting about whether one should drink, are into battles about pouring out the liquor, how can they lay aside the fury of this intense power struggle and make love? So, often anger is also a stumbling block to getting together again sexually when one is sober.

3) Jealousy. It happens that some spouses, usually men, who are impotent because of their drinking, begin to feel suspicious and jealous of their wives without cause. They think they are having affairs with other men. They are angry and accusatory. What happens is that they don't want to accept what alcohol has done to their sexual functioning and they feel that since they are not adequate sexual partners their wives must be getting sex elsewhere. This way, by blaming their wives of infidelity, they are able to avoid looking at their own problem and the way they feel about it.

4) Fear. Many alcoholic people are very frightened by their inability to perform sexually or to feel sexual desire. For men this may mean that they are impotent. For women it may mean that they do not lubricate. They feel they are abnormal not to want sex. What effect does alcohol have on sexual functioning? Studies have shown that in low doses alcohol affects men by delaying ejaculation. This is an effect some men might desire if they wanted to delay their ejaculation. However, in men and women both sexual arousal and sexual performance are interfered with through the use of large amounts of alcohol. Men are made impotent, women do not lubricate.

Studies also show that some men tend to feel more powerful when drinking. Some women tend to feel more sexy and feminine. But what happens is that alcohol is a great deceiver. Just as you think you can walk straight, talk straight, drive straight and be a great lover when you are drunk, it doesn't turn out to be so. The alcohol makes you believe you can. It distorts perception.

How can you tell whether impotence will continue? If men are getting erections at night then they are not physically impotent and the problem is psychological. Sometimes it takes months of abstinence for sexual functioning to return. Sometimes it takes months for sexual desire to return. Time and patience are the most important things to help the problem.

It is all right to say *NO* to something you don't want to do. It is all right not to have intercourse. Start out slowly as with everything else in recovery from alcoholism. Don't expect to function like you did at 18 and if you have been out of practice, it's going to take time to get back in practice.

There's a lot more to sex than intercourse. And who said it was kid stuff? How about masturbation? Some people don't want any part of it. That's all right, too. For those who do, try enjoying it to the fullest, remembering there is kissing, stroking, holding, cuddling, being close. These are all powerful ways to communicate warm feelings other than by having intercourse.

NOTES

1. Carpenter, J.A. and Armenti, N.P., "Some Effects of Ethanol on Human Sexual and Aggressive Behavior," pp. 509-543. In: Kissen, B. and Begleiter, H., eds., *The Biology of Alcoholism, Vol. 2, Physiology and Behavior,* New York, Plenum Press, 1972.

2. Rubin, H.B. and Henson, Donald E., "Effects of Alcoholism on Male Sexual Responding," *Psychopharmacology,* Vol. 47, 1976, pp. 123-124.

3. Farkas, Gary M. and Rosen, C. "Effects of Alcoholism on Elicited Male Sexual Response," *J. Studies Alc.* Vol. 37, No. 3, 1976, pp. 265-271.

4. Wilson, G. Terence and Lawson, David M., "Alcohol and Sexual Arousal in Women," *J. of Abnormal Psychology,* 85, 1976, pp. 489-497.

5. Beckman, Linda J., "Reported Effects of Alcohol on Sexual Feelings and Behavior of Women Alcoholics and Non-alcoholics," *J. Studies Alc.,* Vol. 40, No. 3, 1979, pp. 272-282.

6. Ibid., p. 281.

7. Whalley. L.J.. "Sexual Adjustment of Male Alcoholics." *Acta Psychiat. Scand.* (1978) 58. pp. 281-298.

8. McClelland. D.C. et al.. *The Drinking Man.* New York. Free Press. 1972.

9. Wilsnack. Sharon C.. "The Impact of Sex Roles on Women's Alcohol Use and Abuse." pp. 37-60. In *Alcoholism Problems in Women and Children.* Shuckit and Greenblatt. eds.. Grune & Stratton. 1976.

10. Wilsnack. Sharon C.. "Effects of Social Drinking on Women's Fantasy." *J. of Personality,* Vol. 42. 1974. pp. 43-61.

11. Lemere. Frederick and Smith. James. "Alcohol Induced Sexual Impotence." *Am. J. of Psychiatry,* Vol 130. (1) 1973. pp. 212-214.

12. Sharoff. Robert L.. "Character Problems and Their Relationship to Drug Abuse." *Am. J. of Psychoanalysis,* Vol. 29. 1969-70. pp. 186-193.

13. Masters. William H. and Johnson. Virginia E.. *Human Sexual Inadequacy.* Boston. Little. Brown. 1970. pp. 163-169.

14. Lemere. op cit.. p. 213.

15. Johnson. Vernon. "I'll Quit Tomorrow." Harper and Row. New York. 1973.

16. Paredes. Alfonso. "Marital-sexual Factors in Alcoholism." *Med. Aspects of Human Sexuality,* Vol. 17 (1) April. 1973. pp. 98-114.

17. Silber. Austin. "Rationale for the Technique of Psychotherapy with Alcoholics." *Int. J. of Psychoanal. Psychotherapy* 3:1. pp. 28-47. 1974.

18. Fewell. Christine H. and Bissell. LeClair. "The Alcoholic Denial Syndrome: an Alcohol-focussed Approach." *Social Casework.* January. 1978. pp. 6-13.

Alcoholism in Women:
Current Knowledge and Implications
for Treatment

Shulamith Lala Ashenberg Straussner, M.S.W, A.C.S.W.

ABSTRACT. Alcoholism in women is a problem which is receiving increasing recognition from researchers and practitioners. This paper reviews the growing research findings on alcoholic women and explains how alcoholism in women differs from that in men, and how alcoholic women differ from each other. Treatment implications for dealing with alcoholic women are discussed.

According to an ancient legend, the first person to discover the effect of drinking alcohol was an unnamed woman in the court of the Persian King Jamshid who, feeling depressed, decided to commit suicide by drinking from a jar labeled "poison." This jar initially contained grapes—the King's favorite fruit. However, with the passage of time the grapes fermented and the King was convinced that the strange tasting liquid was poisonous. Fortunately, for the lady, instead of dying from this "poison," she felt happier and after finishing all of the liquid in the jar, fell soundly asleep—probably her first sound sleep in weeks. We don't know if this woman became the first female alcoholic, but, according to the legend, from then on the king deliberately let his grapes ferment and this primitive wine was then served regularly to all the members of the king's court.[57]

In spite of this old legend, the focus on alcohol and women is a relatively recent phenomenon. Drinking, in general, and alcoholism, in particular, have long been considered to be male prerogatives. In his 1972 review of literature, Marc Shuckit found that between 1929 and 1970 *only* twenty nine studies on women alcoholics were published in the English language.[41] Although in the last de-

Acknowledgement: The author wishes to thank Dr. Joel Straussner for all his help and support.

cade the number of studies on alcoholic women has increased greatly, there have been few attempts at a comprehensive summary of the current state of knowledge.[2] Yet, alcoholic women are to be found among our clients, their spouses and mothers, and, as recent findings indicate, among our friends and professional colleagues.[5]

The purpose of this paper is to review the recent findings on alcoholic women and point out their implications for treatment.

It is, however, important to keep in mind that almost all of our present knowledge about alcoholism in women is based on women in treatment who may not necessarily represent alcoholic women in the general population.

INCIDENCE AND PREVALENCE
OF ALCOHOLISM AMONG WOMEN

Reliable national incidence and prevalence studies of alcoholism in women are currently non-existent. Thus, the cited estimates regarding the number of female alchoholics vary tremendously, with figures ranging from less than one million[2] to over five million women.[30] The most commonly accepted estimates for the number of alcoholic women in America range from 1.5 to 2.25 million.[50] However, since the percentage of teenage girls and young women who drink alcoholic beverages has been increasing in recent years,[?] the pool from which future female alcoholics may develop is also growing. Thus, it is crucial to increase our knowledge and understanding of this long neglected, and yet, not uncommon problem population.

Recent research studies on alcoholic women point to growing evidence that alcoholism in women differs from that in men, and, moreover, that alcoholic women differ greatly from each other. These differences are explicated below.

DIFFERENCES BETWEEN MALE
AND FEMALE ALCOHOLICS

Researchers have found that alcoholic men and women differ on a number of variables including etiological, physiological, psychological and sociological factors.

Etiological Differences

Although most authorities in the field of alcoholism believe that no general theory of etiology of alcoholism or an alcoholic personality type is possible, numerous variables relating to the etiology of alcoholism for both men and women have been mentioned in the literature on alcoholism.

One perennial issue is the contribution of heredity as opposed to social environment on the development of alcoholism. Controlled studies on the effect of heredity on alcoholism show different results for men than women.

Whereas studies on Danish adoptees provided some evidence for a genetic factor in alcoholism in males,[17] a follow up study by the same authors of adopted-out daughters of alcoholics showed that "daughters of alcoholics did not differ from daughters of non-alcoholics with regard to problem drinking, depression, or other psychiatric disorders".[18] The authors agree with the unpublished findings of Theodore Reich that "genetic factors outweigh environmental factors in producing alcoholism in men, but that the opposite is true in women" (18, p. 754). If these findings are confirmed by other studies, they hold significant implications for both prevention and treatment of alcoholism in women.

Although they do not provide the answer to the heredity vs. environment question, numerous studies of alcoholic women in treatment show that women are more likely than men to come from families where there is a history of alcoholism. Researchers have found that rate of alcoholism among the parents of alcoholic women to range from a low of 29%[12] to a high of 56%,[46] whereas the rates cited for alcoholism among the parents of alcoholic males have ranged only from 19%[12] to 35%.[25,27]

While most of the focus in literature has been on the high rates of alcoholism among the fathers of alcoholic women,[55] researchers have also noted higher rates of alcoholism in the mothers and siblings of alcoholic women[29,30] as well as generally higher rates of mental illness in their families of origin,[54] and more disruptive early family life[12] than that experienced by men. As stated by Gomberg:[16] "There is more loss, more alcoholism, more depression and other psychiatric problems in the families of people who become alcoholics than there is among those who do not, and there appears to be more loss, more alcohol, and more familial psychiatric problems among women alcoholics than among men alcoholics" (p. 131).

A review of the literature also indicates that "alcoholism and heavy drinking in women appear more likely to be linked to psychological stress and specific precipitating circumstance or situation than is alcoholism or heavy drinking in men" (3, p. 801). In contrast to men who often drink to "be sociable" or because they "like the taste," women show an escapist type of drinking: They drink because they feel "tense" or "nervous," in order to relax or to "forget worries".[4] Factors such as middle age identity crises or the "empty nest syndrome";[12] pregnancy and/or childbirth;[46] and separation;[53] and loss[10] have all been cited as stresses related to excessive drinking by women. It is important to note, however, that in *no case* did these variables relate to, or account for, the majority of the alcoholic women in these studies. The possibility that women are more likely than men to relate their drinking to a stressful situation in order to "justify" their drinking, as well as the possibility that women are generally more attuned to environmental factors without this necessarily implying causality, needs to be kept in mind in interpreting the above findings.

Other etiological variables cited specifically for alcoholic women (the "need for power" and "unresolved dependency needs" have been used to explain alcoholism in males) include sex-role confusion and sex-role conflicts. While some researchers[52,53] have found alcoholic women to be unconsciously more masculine in their identification when compared to non-alcoholic women, a study comparing alcoholic women with their non-alcoholic biological sisters found no significant differences on various instruments used to measure sex-role identification,[10] while still another study[47] found that alcoholic women scored significantly lower on the MMPI Masculinity-Femininity Scale (Scale 5) than "normal" women reflecting an unconscious self-image of almost stereotypic feminine passivity and submissiveness.

The problem with all studies cited above is that they reflect the behaviors and attitudes of women who are already diagnosed as alcoholics, and thus do not answer the question of whether these self perceptions *resulted in*, or are the *result of* their alcoholism. Only long-term longitudinal studies with sufficient number of female subjects may provide more reliable answers regarding the etiology of alcoholism among women. Such longitudinal studies on females — long a method of studying males — are only now commencing.

Physiological Differences

Because of the difference in their body build, males and females show different physiological responses to alcohol consumption. Since women's bodies have more fatty and less muscle tissues (which are largely composed of water), they tend to absorb alcohol faster and become intoxicated sooner on the same amount of alcohol than men of equivalent body weight.[27] Studies have also shown that the level of sex hormones in the body relates to the effect that alcohol has on a woman. Women have thus been shown to become more readily intoxicated prior to their menstruation than at any other time during the month. Thus depending on her menstrual cycle "a woman may obtain a low blood alcohol level and feel minimal effects from alcohol on one occasion, and then may become very intoxicated and act drunk on another occasion after consuming the same amount of alcohol (27, p. 112). It appears that the numerous attempts in the literature on alcoholism to compare men and women purely on the basis of the quantity of alcohol consumed disregard this important differential *qualitative* effect.

Because of the unpredictable effect which alcohol may have on womens' systems, Jones and Jones[27] have hypothesized that this "may encourage women to modulate their drinking: this modulation may result in women developing tolerance to alcohol at a slower rate than men" (27, p. 113). Thus according to their as yet unproven hypothesis, men show a faster development of tolerance and addiction to alcohol than women. This theory appears, on the surface to contradict the frequently cited research finding (which will be discussed later on) that the development of alcoholism in women is "telescoped."[12,29]

Another important finding of the Jones and Jones[27] studies is that women using birth control pills have an additional complication not experienced by men: since both alcohol and the Pill metabolize in the liver, alcohol remains significantly longer in the body of a woman using oral contraceptives. This finding has obvious implications for the detoxification process of alcoholic women.

Differences in the Progression
and Symptomatology of Alcoholism

The progression of alcoholism in women may also differ from that of men. According to a study of women AA members,[23] symptoms such as "gulping of drinks," "sneaking alcohol," or "surreptitious drinking," as well as "guilt" and "persistent remorse" about drinking, which appear relatively early in the progression of alcoholism in men, develop during the later stages in the drinking careers of women. Even "memory blackouts" which is one of the prealcoholic symptoms in males (in the "prodromal stage") is experienced later by women. Interestingly, the only symptom which occurs (slightly) earlier in women than men—"binge drinking"—is one that is not experienced by many alcoholic women.[51] If the above findings of James[23] are validated in further studies, the commonly used diagnostic criteria based on the development of behavioral symptoms[33] may not be appropriate for diagnosing alcoholism in women and may need to be modified.

Other studies relating to the differences in the progression of alcoholism in males and females indicate that in comparison with men, women generally become problem drinkers at a later age,[4] and that they show a more "telescoped" developmental period of alcoholism reflected in a shorter time period between early problem drinking and late stage symptoms,[12] and a shorter duration of problem drinking before coming to treatment.[30,44] This frequently cited "telescoping hypothesis" has been called into question by Ferrence[13] who feels that researchers have not controlled for sex differences in the definition of heavy drinking, nor have they taken into account the fact that women are more likely to seek help for health problems—and to do so at an earlier stage—than men.

One of the most extensive comparisons of symptoms and behavior between men and women with "drinking problems" was done by Wanberg and Horn.[51] Using a sample of 2300 men and women they found that "in contrast to men, the women more frequently drank at home and alone; on the average they started drinking at an older age; they more frequently drank distilled spirits or wine rather than beer; and they were more likely to be first admissions to the hospital . . ." (52, p.41). On a secondary analyses using a sample of 1657 men and 363 women, Wanberg and Horn[51] noticed that whereas many men tend to be periodic drinkers who drink "only on weekends," women tend to show a more continuous and less periodic drinking pattern. This study also found that women tend to drink at a specific time each day and slept much when drinking. According to the authors "This may be the pattern characterizing the housewife who drinks at home and thus can sleep a great deal. However, there is also indication that the woman who scores high on this factor often works and if so, has been able to hold her job in spite of drinking" (p. 53). Wanberg and Horn made one other interesting observation in their comparison between men and women: While alcoholic women "are more defensive in verbally acknowledging their problem, they are less defensive in actually seeking treatment" (p. 49).

Psychological and Social Differences

Numerous studies indicate that alcoholic women are more likely than alcoholic men to attempt suicide,[12] and to have primary affective disorder.[43,54] Most of the suicide attempts appear to involve overdosing with legally prescribed pills.[47] Some writers have related the high rate of suicide attempts to a higher incidence of primary affective disorder in women with a drinking problem.[44] Figures as high as 27% of primary affective disorder among alcoholic women have been cited.[55] It is important to note that higher rates of suicide attempts and of affective disorders are found in women than men in the general population—a factor that needs to be kept in mind in analyzing the above findings.

Both the use and abuse of pills, especially minor tranquilizers and sedative-hypnotics, tend to be higher among alcoholic women than that found among alcoholic men[12] or among women in the general population.[10] The combination of "a possible greater degree of vulnerability to substance dependency among women alcoholics, and a greater tendency on the part of physicians to prescribe medication" (16, p. 151) results in women running a grave risk of accidental overdosage. This potentially deadly combination must be constantly kept in mind when treating the alcoholic woman.

Possibly due to the still terrible stigma of being a female alcoholic, alcoholism in women is less likely to be identified as such and more likely to be denied or ignored by authorities than is alcoholism in men.

Women have been found less likely than men to be arrested for drunk driving,[36] even though one study has found that a higher percentage of women than men admitted to driving while under the influence of alcohol.[8] However, the number of women who have trouble with the police due to their drinking may be higher than previously thought. A recent study by Corrigan[10] of alcoholic women admitted to 14 treatment facilities found that 28% of these women of various socioeconomic backgrounds "had contacts with the police on offenses related to their drinking" (p. 74). Nevertheless, even if women have "contact" with the police, they do not necessarily get arrested, and, once arrested, have been shown to be more likely to be represented by a lawyer and subsequently less likely than men to be jailed and/or referred to treatment by the courts.[9] Similarly, preliminary studies comparing alcoholic men and women in the workplace found that alcoholic women are less likely to be confronted and referred for help by their supervisors than alcoholic men.[31]

This greater tendency toward denial of alcoholism in women than in men also extends to their families[47] and friends, and even to the helping professionals.

Differences in Treatment Outcomes

The issue of treatment outcome for alcoholic women as compared to alcoholic men has received some attention although valid research data are scarce. Many research studies focus on treatment outcome for "alcoholics" or "problem drinkers" without specifying if the data relates to men, women or both. Furthermore, as noted by Blume[8] "many of the best controlled studies on treatment involving substantial numbers of patients have come out of the Veterans Administration, a practically all-male treatment system" (8 p. 33). Although several studies have found that males have better treatment outcome than females,[12,37] other studies showed the outcome to be equal[14,45] or even better for women.[10] A recent study of treatment-related differences for male and female clients of New York State's system of alcoholic rehabilitation units found an almost equal proportion of men (61%) and women (60%) reporting abstinence at an eight month follow up,[41] while in her study of 116 alcoholic women, Corrigan[10] found a 41% rate of total abstinence and an additional 12% of women who drank only "on a rare occasion" 13 months after admission to treatment. These figures surpass most of the recovery rates reported for men during a similar time frame.

It appears likely that the recovery rate for women varies depending on such factors as primary pathology and socio-economic class. It is also possible that just as the progression of alcoholism in women may differ from that in men, so may the process of recovery. A study of 50 alcoholic housewives by Straussner et al.[46] found that 38% of these women had periods of sobriety ranging from almost one year to over 8 years before they resumed drinking. It may be that women abstain for longer periods before "slip-

ping"—but are then more likely than men to seek professional help
once they do drink. This area needs further study.

DIFFERENCES AMONG ALCOHOLIC WOMEN

Researchers have reported that there is relatively greater variability or heterogeneity among women alcoholics than among men. According to Gomberg "This may be a reflection of women's greater
variability in all things. Her life is more differentiated by physiological shifts into stages than is a man's, and the choice of roles offered
the contemporary woman as wife, mother, wage earner, careerist,
community activist and so on is wider" (16, p. 139). Thus, it is important not only to examine the differences between alcoholic men
and women, but also among alcoholic women.

Differences Related to Differential Diagnosis

One valuable area of research has focused on distinguishing
women with primary alcoholism from those for whom alcoholism is
secondary to affective disorder.[42,43] According to Schuckit,[42] alcoholic women with primary affective disorder tend to be younger,
have a shorter duration of alcoholism and, in spite of more suicide
attempts, have a better treatment prognosis. These findings may account for the conflicting findings regarding treatment outcomes for
alcoholic women since those studies did not take this differential diagnosis and prognosis into account.

Differences Related to Socio-Economic Status

Another useful distinction among alcoholic women is based on
the difference in socio-economic status. Although there are more
abstainers among poor women than among middle or upper income
women,[28] those poor women who drink have a higher rate of alcoholism and their drinking pattern resembles more the drinking of
men than that of women of higher socio-economic class.

Researchers have found that alcoholic women of higher socio-
economic status have a later age of onset of alcoholism, are older
when they get to treatment, drink less alcohol, are less likely to report binge or morning drinking, and are less likely to suffer from alcohol related problems such as physical illness, suicidal behavior,

arrests, and loss of friends or jobs due to drinking.[21] In contrast, women of lower socioeconomic class experience more childhood and marital disruption, more erratic employment histories, more familial alcoholism and are more prone to bout drinking than other women.[20] They are also less likely to drink alone, or to hide their drinking from others.[10] While women of higher socio-economic class tend to seek treatment for family or marital problems, women from lower socio-economic groups are more likely to come to treatment because of job problems.

The probability of an alcoholic woman being married to an alcoholic man also varies depending on her socio-economic class. Researchers have found the rates of alcoholic husbands to vary from as low as 8% among middle and upper socio-economic class,[56] to as high as 56% among lower class alcoholic women.[29]

Overall, it appears that alcoholism among lower class women may be socially induced, while among middle class women it may be related more to psychological factors. This hypothesis needs to be explored further.

Differences Related to Employment Status

Although working women, regardless of socio-economic status, show higher rates of heavier and problem drinking than housewives,[50] research on alcoholism among female workers and especially among professional women is only now beginning to be done and has yet to be widely published.

It has been reported, however, that it is the married, working woman—the modern "superwoman" trying to juggle both family and work responsibilities—who is most likely to abuse alcohol.[26]

Differences Related to Sexual Preference

Although clinical impression exists that alcoholism is prevalent among the homosexual community, no systematic research of alcoholic lesbians has been conducted. Although figures of 20% to 35% rate of alcoholism among homosexuals have been cited in several articles and books reviewed,[21,22,43,57] the validity of these figures seems questionable since they may not be generalizable outside of their sample population. A statistical calculation of 2-1/2% rate of alcoholism among lesbians has been proposed by Hawkins[29] who also feels that "the influence of the bar scene on the homosexual community contributes significantly to the abuse of alcohol, even though the bar is predominantly for socialization" (20 p. 149). Accurate prevalence rates, other possible etiological variables, and the treatment needs of this doubly stigmatized population await further study.

Differences Related to Aging

Another group of women which needs to be studied further is the elderly alcoholic female. One study of English geriatric population found that elderly women with drinking problems outnumbered elderly men with drinking problems, even after taking into account the larger number of women in the general elderly population.[39] This does not appear to be true in the United States where it has been estimated that only two percent of the older female population are heavy or problem drinkers in contrast to ten percent of elderly males.[49] However, the fact that there are more elderly women than men in the general population indicates that alcoholism among elderly females is a significant problem that needs to be recognized.

Although many facilities are reluctant to admit the elderly alcoholic, either male or female, studies have shown that elderly people who become alcoholics late in life have a better response to treatment than those who were alcoholics in their early years.[50]

Differences Related to Minority Status

Studies on black women alcoholics are scarce, even though alcoholism in the black urban community is considered the number one health problem.[22] As early as 1942, Jellinek noted that the mortality rate for alcoholism in blacks was higher than that in whites and that the high black rate was due primarily to very high rates among black *women*.[24] The 1965 New York City Household Survey showed a much closer ratio (1.9 to 1) of black alcoholic males to females than that found in comparing white males to females (6.2 to 1).[1] Moreover, in their 1965 National Survey of American Drinking Practice, Cahalan and Cisin[11] observed that while the proportion of drinking among black men varied little from that of white men, black women showed both a higher proportion of abstainers (51% vs. 39%) and heavy drinkers (11% vs. 4%) than white women. Among the explanations posited for these findings are (1) that black women are more likely to be found in low income levels which have been found to show high patterns of both abstinence and alcoholism, and (2) that black women are more likely to be heads of households, and that a higher proportion of alcoholism is related to more frequent head of household status.[1] However, in a 1972 survey of an all Black, low-income housing project in St. Louis done by Sterne and Pittman, it was found that "female heavy drinkers are not significantly more likely than other women who drink to be household heads, workers, or generally more impoverished" (15, p. 159).

Studies on treatment outcomes for black women also show conflicting findings. In a 1961 study of black patients admitted to a Connecticut mental hospital, Strayer noted that the treatment success for black women was greater than that shown for black men or white women.[47] Corrigan[10] however, found that in comparison to white women, her black female subjects showed significant lower rates of both abstinence (50% for white vs. 13% for black women) and a lower rate of reduction to the "rare-occasion" drinking pattern (63% vs. 22%). Corrigan notes that "clearly the black women have considerably fewer supports for a change in drinking: many continue to live in a setting whose heavy drinking is the custom and to lack a supportive network of friends and family" (10, p. 141). One important supportive network for a recovering alcoholic is AA. In her correlation of drinking outcomes, emotional health scores and treatment, Corrigan states that "AA treatment combined with either inpatient or outpatient treatment shows 39% now abstaining as compared with the 15% who did not have AA treatment" (10, p. 149). Although Corrigan does not connect these two above observations, it appears (based on my own observations) that black women are less likely than white women to utilize AA and thus lack one very important support in their recovery process.

Studies on the drinking patterns and prevalance of alcoholism among Hispanic women are almost non-existent, although recently there has been a growing interest in the drinking patterns among the Chicano community in California.[32] Although most experts agree that the percentage of Hispanic women who drink is low in comparison to both black and white women,[29] the alcoholic Puerto Rican woman appears to be the most underrepresented in treatment facilities of all women. In her sample of 150 women from 14 North-Eastern treatment facilities, Corrigan[10] found only 5 Puerto Rican women, while Straussner et al.[46] found only 7 Puerto Rican women in a population of 788 women treated over a four year period in a New York City rehab center. (In both of these studies, black women comprised over a quarter of the female population.) The lack of Hispanic women in treatment has been explained by the "double standard" which is so strong among Latin culture: unlike their men, women are not supposed to drink. Thus, "Latin women who drink may be under a double mandate—not to reveal their drinking and not to seek help—that is even more compelling than the cultural prohibitions against the use of alcohol" (32, p. 104).

EFFECTS OF ALCOHOLISM ON WOMAN'S FERTILITY AND OFFSPRING

No discussion on alcoholic women would be complete without some mention of the effect of drinking on a woman's fertility and her offspring. While several researchers have found excessive infertility among alcoholic women,[51] a recent study on alcoholic housewives found only a 10% rate of infertility among these long-married females.[46] This figure is within the norm of infertile couples in the United States. It may be that women who are infertile are more likely to be divorced and less likely to be found among a population of married housewives. This area needs further research.

While many alcoholic women report that they tend spontaneously to reduce their drinking once they become pregnant, studies of offsprings of those women who continue to drink heavily during their pregnancies show increasing evidence of birth defects and behavioral impairments in their children. The fetal alcohol syndrome— a recently recognized pattern of growth deficiency, altered morphogenesis, and mental impairment—that has been found in some children whose mothers drank heavily during pregnancy, was first identified in France in 1968.[49] Studies in the United States done over the last seven years have shown the fetal alcohol syndrome to be the third leading congenital disorder—following Down's Syndrome and Spina Bifida—associated with mental retardation. More significantly, it is the only one of the three that is preventable. Experts also believe that maternal alcohol use may be a contributing factor in what has been termed minimal brain dysfunction—a pattern of abnormalities of attention, behavior and learning problems affecting five to seven million children in the United States today.[50]

TREATMENT IMPLICATIONS

In order to treat the alcoholic woman, the worker needs not only a thorough knowledge of alcoholism, but also a sensitivity to the issues specific to women.

Because of the tendency in our society to deny alcoholism in a woman, workers must be vigilant about their own tendency toward such denial. Questions about drinking history and the effect of a woman's drinking on her physical, mental health, and on her every day functioning, should be a standard component of every diagnostic interview regardless of the setting or presenting problem. The previously cited physiological factors, as well as socio-economic and minority status differences should be taken into account when diagnosing or treating the alcoholic woman.

In diagnosing or treating a woman, the worker should not use the quantity of her alcohol consumption as a diagnostic criteria. As research findings indicate, a woman need not drink as much as a man to be an alcoholic and to suffer serious mental and physical consequences. Moreover, it is crucial that treatment staff working with an alcoholic woman take not only a good drinking history, but also be knowledgeable about her pill history. Because of the high probability of her use and abuse of tranquilizers and sedative-hypnotic drugs, the woman abusing alcohol needs education about cross-addiction, cross-tolerance, and the synergistic, and frequently deadly, effect of combining alcohol and pills. The alcoholic woman with a history of pill abuse may require a longer detoxification and treatment process; she and her family should be prepared for such possibility from the very beginning.

By the time a woman seeks treatment for alcoholism, most likely she has already been seen by her family physician, by a psychiatrist, possibly by a marriage counselor or minister, all of whom may have unknowingly colluded with her own denial of alcoholism. She is weary and wants to feel better, yet is mistrustful—having been misdiagnosed and mismedicated in the past—of those who are offering help. Frequently, she feels a tremendous sense of guilt and shame, at the same time feeling victimized and full of rage at those around her.[46]

In order to effectively help the alcoholic woman, the treatment staff must guide her in identifying her problem and recognize her probable low sense of self-esteem, feelings of depression, hopelessness, and helplessness. The alcoholic woman needs help in seeing her own role in her victimization, and in learning how to muster her resources to help herself. Through the use of such techniques as assertiveness training, role playing, and didactic lectures, the alcoholic woman can learn that there are better ways of dealing with her feelings of anger, resentment, self-pity, and depression than taking a drink or a pill. Whether in her concern about her problem children, her aging parents, or the demands of her husband or lover, the alcoholic woman needs guidance in how to remain responsive to the needs of her loved ones, yet retain her own identity and place her sobriety first. Whether through AA, peer discussions, individual, or group therapy, the alcoholic woman will benefit from having access to a successful role-model with whom she can identify.

The alcoholic woman will often need concrete help in arranging for child care before she can go into a hospital or attend an AA meeting or a therapy session. Furthermore, since so many alcoholic women are married to alcoholic men, the woman will also need help in evaluating her ability to stay sober in such a relationship. It is not uncommon for the husband or boy-friend, whether alcoholic or not, to resent and be jealous of a woman's AA involvement during her early sobriety. Using such treatment modalities as family therapy, group, or individual sessions, help needs to be offered to those significant people in the life of the alcoholic woman. They all can also benefit from referrals to AlAnon and AlAteen.

There is no denying that alcoholism has a tremendous effect on women, their families, and society. It is thus extremely important that those working with, or concerned about, the alcoholic woman learn about the special characteristics and treatment needs of women alcoholics.

REFERENCE NOTES

1. Bailey, M.B., Haberman, P.W., and Alksne, H. "The Epidemiology of Alcoholism in an Urban Residential Area." *Quart. Jr. Stud. Alcohol* 26: 19-23, 1965.

2. Babcock, M. and Connor, V. "Sexism and Treatment of the Female Alcoholic: A Review." *Social Work*, 26: 233-238, 1981.

3. Beckman, L.J. "Women Alcoholics: A Review of Social and Psychological Studies." *J.Stud Alc 36*: 797-824, 1975.

4. Beckman, L.J. "Alcoholism Problems and Women: An Overview." in *Alcoholism Problems in Women and Children*. Greenblatt, M. & M.A. Schuckit, eds, New York: Grune & Stratton, 1976.

5. Bissell, L., Fewell, C., and Jones, R. "The Alcoholic Social Worker: A Survey." *Social Work and Health Care*, Vol. 5 (4): 421-432, 1980.

6. Blume, S. "Researches on Women and Alcohol: Diagnosis, Casefinding, Treatment and Outcome." Topic Paper prepared for NIAAA Workshop on Alcoholism and Alcohol Abuse Among Women, Jekyll Island, Georgia April, 1978.

7. Blackford, Lillian St. Clair. "Summary Report: Survey of Student Drug Use San Mateo, Calif.," 1977. Mimeograph Copy.

8. Blume, S. "Diagnosis, Casefinding and Treatment of Alcohol Problems in Women." *Alcohol Health and Research World*, 2(3), Fall, 1978.

9. Blumenthal, M. and Ross, H. "Two Experimental Studies of Traffic Law. Vol. I, *The Effect of Legal Sanctions on DWI Offenders*, Dept. of Transportation, 1973 cited in Blume, S. "Researches on Women and Alcohol" 1978.

10. Corrigan, E.M. *Alcoholic Women in Treatment*, New York: Oxford University Press, 1980.

11. Cahalan, D. and Cisin, I. "American Drinking Practices: Summary of Findings From a National Probability Sample." *Q. Jr. Stu. Alc.* 29: 130-151, 1968.

12. Curlee, J. "A Comparison of Male and Female Patients At an Alcoholism Treatment Center." *J. Psychol*, 74: 239-247, 1970.

13. Ferrence, R. "Women and Alcohol: Current Knowledge and Persisting Myths." *The Journal*, Feb. 1, 1980, p. 9.

14. Fitzgerald, B.J., Pasewark, P.A. and Clark, R. "Four Year Follow Up of Alcoholics Treated at a Rural State Hospital." *Quart Jr. Stu. Alc.* 32: 636-642, 1971.

15. Gaines, J.J. "Alcohol and the Black Woman" in *Alcohol Abuse and Black America*. Harper, F.D. ed., Washington, D.C.: Douglass Publishers, Inc., 1976.

16. Gomberg, E.S. "Alcoholism in Women" in *Social Aspects of Alcoholism*, Kissin, B. and H. Begleiter, Eds., New York: Plenum Press, 1976.

17. Goodwin, D.W., Schulsinger, F. and Hermansen, L. "Alcohol Problems in Adoptees Raised Apart From Alcoholic Biological Parents." *Arch. of Gen. Psyh*, 28: 238-243, 1973.

18. Goodwin, D.W., Schulsinger, F., Knop, J. Mendick, S. and Guze, S. "Alcoholism and Depression in Adopted-Out Daughters of Alcoholics." *Arch. of Gen. Psych*, 34: 751-755, 1977.

19. Haberman, P.W. "Denial of Drinking in Household Survey." *Q. Jr. Stud Alcoh.*, 31: 710-717, 1970.

20. Hawkins, J.L. "Lesbianism and Alcoholism" in *Alcohol Problems in Women and Children*. Greenblatt, M. and M. Schuckit, eds. New York: Grune & Stratton, 1976.

21. Homiller, J.D. *Women and Alcohol: A Guide for State and Local Decision Makers*. ADPA, Washington, D.C. 1977.

22. Hornik, E.L. *The Drinking Woman*, New York: Association Press, 1970.

23. James J.E. "Symptoms of Alcoholism in Woman, A Preliminary Survey of AA Members." *J.Stu. Al.*, 36: 1564-1569, 1975.

24. Jellinek, E.M. "Death From Alcoholism in the United States in 1940: A Statistical Analysis." *Q.J. Stud. Alc.*, 3:365-370, 1942.

25. Jellinek, E.M. "Heredity of the Alcoholic." *Alcohol, Science and Society: Twenty-Nine Lectures*, New Haven, *Q.J. Stud. Alcoh.*, 1945.

26. Johnson, P., Armor, D.J., Polich, S. and Stambul, H., U.S. Adult Drinking Practices: Time Trends, Social Correlates and Sex Roles. Santa Monica, Calif. Rand Corp. 1977.

27. Jones, B.M. & M.K. Jones. "Women and Alcohol: Intoxication, Metabolism, and the Menstrual Cycle" in *Alcoholism Problems in Women and Children*. Greenblatt and Schuckit, eds., New York: Grune & Stratton, 1976.

28. Lawrence, J.J. and Maxwell, M.A. "Drinking and Socio-Economic Status" in *Society, Culture and Drinking Patterns*, Pittman, D.J. & D.R. Snyde eds., New York: Wiley, 1962.

29. Lisansky, E.S. "Alcoholism in Women: Social and Psychological Concomitants, I. Social History Data." *Q.Jr. Stud. Alcoh.*, 16: 675-680, 1955.

30. Lisansky, E.S. "The Woman Alcoholic," *Annals of The American Academy of Political and Social Science*, 315: 73-81, 1958.

31. Levy, Marguerite F. "Alcoholic Women in Industry: Some Empirical Data" paper presented at the 1980 Annual Alcoholism Institute of the NYC Chapter, NASW.

32. Lopez-Lee, D. "Alcoholism Among Third World Women: Research and Treatment"

in *Women Who Drink: Alcoholic Experience and Psychotherapy*, V. Burtle, Ed., Springfield: Charles C. Thomas, 1979.

33. National Council on Alcoholism Criteria Committee, "Criteria for the Diagnosis of Alcoholism," *Annals of Internal Medicine*. 77:125-137, 1972.

34. New York City Affiliate—National Council on Alcoholism, "Facts on Alcoholism and Women."

35. Parker, F. B. "Sex-Role Adjustment in Women Alcoholics," *Q. Jr. Stud. 33*: 647–652, 1972.

36. Pastor, P. "The Control of Public Drunkenness: A Comparison of Legal and Medical Models," Unpublished Doctoral Dissertation, Yale Univ., Dept. of Sociol, 1975, cited in Schuckit & Morrissey "Alcoholism in Women: Some Clinical and Social Perspectives" in *Alcoholism Problems in Women and Children*, 1976.

37. Pemberton, D.A. "A Comparison of the Outcome of Treatment in Female and Male Alcoholics," *British Jr. of Psych., 113*: 367-373, 1967.

38. Roman, P. and Trice, H. "Alcohol Abuse and Work Organizations" in *Social Aspects of Alcoholism*, Dissin & Begleiter, Eds., New York: Plenum Press, 1976.

39. Rosin, A.J. and Glatt, M.M., "Alcohol Excess in the Elderly," *Qr. Jr. Stud. Alc., 32*: 53-61, 1971.

40. Schuckit, M.A. and Winokur, G. "A Short Term Follow Up of Women Alcoholics," *Dis. Nerv. Syst., 33*: 672-678, 1972.

41. Schuckit, M. "The Alcoholic Woman: A Literature Review," *Psychiatry in Medicine, 3*: 37-43, 1972.

42. Schuckit, M., Pitts, F.N., Reich, T., King, L.J. and Winokur, G. "Alcoholism I: Two Types of Alcoholism in Women:, *Arch. Gen Psych., 20*: 301-306, 1969.

43. Schuckit, M.A. and Morrisey, E.R. "Alcoholism in Women: Some Clinic and Social Perspectives with an Emphasis on Possible Subtypes" in *Alcoholism Problems in Women and Children*, Greenblatt and Schuckit, ed. New York: Grune & Stratton, 1976.

44. Sclare, A.B. "The Female Alcoholic:, *British Jr. of Addiction, 65*: 99-107, 1970.

45. Sokolow, L., Welte, J., Hynes, G. and Lyons, J. "Treatment Related Differences Between Female and Male Alcoholics," *Focus on Women, 1*: 42-57, 1980.

46. Straussner, S.L.A., Kitman, C., Straussner, J. & Demos, E. "The Alcoholic Housewife: A Psychosocial Analysis of 50 Self-Defined Housewives," *Focus on Women, 1*: 5-31, 1980.

47. Straussner, S.L.A., Weinstein, D. and Hernandez, R. "Effect of Alcoholism on The Family System," *Health and Social Work, 4*: 112-127, 1979.

48. Strayer, P. "A Study of the Negro Alcoholic," *Q.Jr. Stud. Alc., 22*: 111-123, 1961.

49. Stressguth, A.P. "Maternal Alcoholism and the Outcome of Pregnancy: A Review of Fetal Alcohol Syndrome" in *Alcoholism Problems in Women and Children*, Greenblatt & Schuckit, eds., 1976.

50. U.S. Dept. of Health, Education and Welfare, *Third Special Report To The U.S. Congress on Alcohol and Health*, June, 1978.

51. Wanberg, K.W. and Horn, J.L. "Alcoholism Symptom Patterns of Men and Women: A Comparative Study," *Q. Jr. Stud. Alcoh., 31*: 40-61, 1970.

52. Wilsnack, S.C. "Sex-Role Identity in Female Alcoholism," *Jr. of Abnormal Psych., 82*: 253-261, 1973.

53. Wilsnak, S.C. "The Impact of Sex Roles on Women's Alcohol Use and Abuse" in *Alcoholism Problems in Women and Children*, Greenblatt & Schuckit, Eds., 1976.

54. Winokur, G. and Clyton, P. "Family History Studies, IV. Comparison of Male and Female Alcoholics," *Q. Jr. Stud. Alcoh. 29*: 885–891, 1968.

55. Winokur, G., Reich, T., Rimmer, J. and Pitts, F.N. "Alcoholism III: Diagnosis and Familial Psychiatric Illness in 259 Alcoholic Probands," *Arch. of Gen. Psych., 23*: 104-111, 1970.

56. Wood, H.P. and Duffy, E.L. "Psychological Factors in Alcoholic Women," *Amer. Jr. Psych., 123*: 341–345, 1966.

57. Youcha, G., *A Dangerous Pleasure*. New York: Hawthorne Books, Inc. 1978.

Theoretical Concerns
in the Clinical Treatment
of Substance-Abusing Women:
A Feminist Analysis

Margaret Nichols, Ph.D.

ABSTRACT. This paper examines female alcohol and prescription drug misuse from a socio-political prospective and offers treatment suggestions based on these theoretical assumptions. It demonstrates how women's roles in society, reflecting the existence of sexism and female oppression, affects the patterns and types of chemicals women abuse, as well as their subsequent treatment. Feminist counseling is proposed as an effective approach for female substance misusers.

For many years, it was a truism in the mental health field that "men drink, women get depressed." Now it appears that women drink as well as get depressed: while men still drink more than women, the percentage of female drinkers has risen since World War II, and the number of female adolescents who drink, in particular, has risen dramatically.[25] If we look at individuals who abuse other "legal" substances besides alcohol—prescription and over-the counter pills—women clearly outnumber men.[19] And dual addiction of alcohol and pill abuse is a strikingly common female pattern,[17] suggesting that pill and alcohol use among women are nearly interchangeable. Most importantly, professionals who work with alcoholics and pill abusers are recognizing that male and female substance abusers have different problems with differing etiology and different treatment needs.

This paper will take a broad view of female alcohol and pill abuse and show that this problem has socio-political roots in sexism and the oppression of women. It will demonstrate that on a social level the very patterns and types of chemicals women abuse have been shaped by their roles in society. On an individual etiologic level, available data will be described that show that female substance abusers experience role conflicts of various sorts and/or have disproportionately been victims of sexual assault. Further, it will be suggested that the consequences of alcoholism/pill abuse for women —the way they are treated *after* they develop problems—is determined by sexism. Finally, the paper will make tentative suggestions for the clinical treatment of women based upon these theoretical assumptions.

The reader should understand that this position is a radical and controversial one. This is not only because it is a feminist position, but also because it is a *political* analysis of a problem in a field that is disease-model oriented. And my feminist analysis, while rather unique in the alcoholism field, derives from viewpoints that are at least ten years old in the mental health field and that are, if not exactly mainstream, certainly respectable and not particularly shocking.

SOCIETAL PATTERNS OF FEMALE SUBSTANCE ABUSE

Women's problems with psychoactive chemical abuse in this country appear to have begun with the Industrial Revolution; the growth of female alcoholism in significant numbers is probably much more recent.[1-3] It is important to recognize the extent to which, right from the beginning, women's use of pills was connected to role conflict. Before the Industrial Revolution, in fact, the female role of housewife/mother as we know it simply didn't exist. Prior to the advent of marketplace economy, women were primarily producers of household goods, from soap to clothing, and managers of the house. Child-care was not a major part of woman's work, being left to older siblings, nor was housecleaning (in fact, the term "spring cleaning" originally referred to the *one time per year* the house was cleaned!). The female role as we know it—confined to private versus public life, isolated, restricted to housework and child-care—is only about one hundred years old. And right from the time this role became the prevalent norm for women, it made women "ill."[1]

This occurred, in part, because changes in women's roles took place at the same time as did changes in the role of physicians in our culture. As the Industrial Revolution progressed, more and more household goods began to be produced by small manufacturers rather than by women on their farms and in their households, and as the robust, important role of women shrank to its current more menial role, the middle-class woman expected to live this new life of comparative comfort grew more and more depressed, expressing her malaise at that time through hypochondriacal and hysterical symptoms.[11] This development—the emergence of female "mental illness" as a widespread phenomenon—coincided with the development of the "physician class" in this country, i.e., the elevation of physicians from a profession of no more status than, say blacksmiths, to the profession's current exalted social position.

Middle-class housewives with hysterical/hypochondriacal complaints—the same women Freud studied in Europe—became physicians' first patients in this country.[11] In one way, the combination was perfect: these women were relatively docile and tractable and were certainly long-term patients, and the new physicians needed manageable patients. But in another sense these women presented dilemmas to doctors: they couldn't be cured. As a consequence, out of the need to achieve success, doctors began to prescribe tonics and patent medicines containing opiate drugs and/or cocaine, and eventually to prescribe pure morphine itself. In fact, by the turn of this century there were one million opiate addicts in this country, more than there ever have been since—virtually all of these were white, middle-class housewives "hooked" by their doctors.[10]

We must remember that at that time drinking was a primarily *male* phenomenon; it is probably partially true that opiates were more acceptable for women because opiate effects were more subdued and less obvious than alcohol effects. But on the whole, the pattern of gender and substance abuse found at the turn of the century reflects that which exists today: more women than men use prescribed drugs, more men than women use illegal drugs and alcohol.[13,8]

This effect is so pronounced throughout our history, in fact, that when in 1918 the Harrison Act made opiate drugs *illegal*, an amazing thing happened: women stopped taking drugs! For a time, women seemed relatively free of either significant alcoholism or drug problems. But during the first half of this century pharmaceutical science perfected a host of psychoactive substances that were available in pill form: tranquilizers, barbiturates, stimulants. At first used with hospitalized psychiatric patients, these chemicals soon began to be used on an outpatient basis, again, prescribed to women more than men. Women, primarily housewives, receive over two-thirds the prescriptions for psychoactive drugs in this country; this year, more than one third of all women over thirty in the country will get at least one prescription for a mood-altering drug.[8,13,5]

Why is prescription drug use so common among women? To some extent, it is clearly *iatrogenic,* or physician-induced. Studies of physicians' attitudes toward female patients show that (mostly male) doctors regard their female patients as "complaining" and "hysterical" and that they prescribe psychoactive drugs in response to these perceptions; moreover, drug industry advertising caters to this view of women.[8,18] But it is probably also true that prescription drug use is related to depression, which is endemic to women.[21,23] It is by now well-known that women exhibit higher rates of "mental disorder" than do men, while men show more socially deviant behavior (criminality, alcoholism, heroin addiction)[16,15,6] Of the mental disorders exhibited by women, depression is most prevalent, and is especially high among married housewives. To a large extent, prescription drug abuse among women is probably a response to depression: medication and particularly self-medication.

Thus, viewing the over-all patterns of female chemical use, several features become obvious:

(1) Women tend to use legal, socially-sanctioned substances. In this culture, the sexes tend to respond to stress differentially: men are "bad" (act out in socially deviant ways); women are "mad" (develop "mental disorders"). Even in terms of chemical use and abuse, women tend to use "medicine" while men "get high."

(2) Women's pill use is probably related to depression. Depression, in turn, has clearly been related to woman's role as married housewife.[23,2] Depression and its concomitant prescription drug use seem to be the reaction to the pressures of the female role.

(3) To some extent, female chemical use and abuse is iatrogenic, or physician-induced. Ironically, women are introduced to chemical use through their trusting dependence upon a male.

If this is the case, then what are we to make of female alcohol abusers? Are the roots of women's alcohol abuse *different* from the roots of female pill abuse; and female alcoholics more like male alcoholics than they are like female pill users?

An analysis of the trends in female drinking patterns suggests that in fact female alcoholics closely resemble female pill users. Since World War II, women's consumption of alcohol has risen more rapidly than men's, but not necessarily because of emancipation. The Camberwell Council on Alcoholism[4] suggest several reasons for this increase: drinking has become more socially acceptable for women; alcohol has become available in supermarkets; and the liquor industry has geared special campaigns towards women, especially in the sale of wine and cordials, which women drink disproportionately. In other words, women drink more now not because they are more adventurous, more socially deviant, but because drinking has become *less* deviant for women and more accessible to the housewife. Moreover, the drinking patterns of female alcoholics differ markedly from men's: they tend to be housewives who drink alone at home;[14] they tend to perceive their alcohol use as self-medication in reaction to life stress[4] and they tend to have predisposing affective disorders of depression.[25] Finally, while female alcohol use is not physician-induced, it does tend to be related to the woman's dependency upon a man: the Rand Report[1] found that 35% of female alcoholics and 63% of female problem drinkers had alcoholic spouses, and many had been introduced to drinking by these spouses.

In summary, then, we see that women's substance abuse is shaped by social forces of sexism: women tend to use socially-acceptable substances in response to depression generated by the female role, and their introduction to these substances is often through a male, either their spouse or physician.

INDIVIDUAL CHARACTERISTICS OF FEMALE ABUSERS

We have already discussed some of the important individual characteristics of women who abuse pills and alcohol: that they tend to be married housewifes, that they tend to be solitary, at-home users and drinkers, that they more often report their substance abuse to be a form of medication in response to a life stress; that they tend to have histories of depression that pre-date their chemical abuse.[25] Another is that lesbianism or early sexual trauma such as rape or incest are often concomitants of chemical abuse.[13,25] In addition, women tend to seek treatment over distress that their chemical abuse has caused within their families, while male alcoholics more often seek treatment because of job-related difficulties.[14] And finally, it seems that sex-role conflict has been found frequently in both male and female alcoholics.[24,12] Female chemical abusers, in particular, tend to be *strongly identified* with traditional sex roles (desiring 4.15 children, for example, as compared to 2.94 reported by controls).[24] They are, however, unable to make these traditional roles "work" for them—they are disappointed by these roles—and it is hypothesized that the resultant depression and internalized anger is "medicinally" alleviated through chemical abuse.[14]

If we look at this picture, what do we see? We see that female chemical abusers tend to idealize the female role, to be overly conventional. They are, however, unable to be happy in this role; they may be stigmatized from this role and simply not fit by virtue of lesbianism or early sexual trauma that makes them feel shame. They may feel inadequate in this role because of sexual or reproductive dysfunction. Or they may simply come to feel disappointed in the traditional role of housewife and mother, especially if, as is often the case, they are married to alcoholic spouses. Because of their conventional values, however, their discontent may be expressed as depression rather than a healthy rebellion. And they can alleviate that depression through pills obtained from a physician and/or alcohol obtained from an alcoholic spouse. Finally, they will seek treatment because the alternative they sought to alleviate their role-conflict induced distress produces problems in that very role, in their family. In short, we see that, in an individual, one prevalent pattern of substance abuse among women revolves around conflict over the female role: traditional adherence to this role often coupled with conditions that make it impossible for the woman to live up to or find fulfillment in the role.

THE CONSEQUENCES OF SUBSTANCE ABUSE BY WOMEN

Just as *social acceptability* of various substances determines the frequency with which women will use different psychoactive chemicals, so does social acceptability determine the sequellae of chemical use of women.

The woman who abuses legal, prescription drugs is largely tolerated and ignored in this society; most people will not even consider her to have a problem. Thus, even though 17% of women in this country are dependent upon a prescription psychoactive drug,[1] and despite the fact that Valium is now the leading drug overdose seen in hospital emergency rooms, with 73% of victims women,[22] few women using legal psychoactive substances are ever singled out for help. Indeed, the consequences of "pill abuse"—when not combined with alcohol abuse—are probably less tangible than the repercussions of alcohol or illegal drug abuse. Few legal drugs have the devastating physical effects associated with alcohol, nor do they have the social consequences (criminality, etc.) of illicit chemicals. While many are addictive,[7] their addiction and habituation patterns tend to be more stable than patterns for, say, alcohol use, so that constant levels of use can sometimes be maintained for many years. If we assume that the women who seek these drugs are attempting to stabilize disquieting role conflicts, then it appears that a major effect of these chemicals is to "help" women maintain their roles as housewives and parents: "Mother's little helpers." Indeed, apart from the as-yet-unknown percentage of risk that these women will become alcoholic,* the major negative consequences of prescription pill use by women are personal quality-of-life issues and socio-political consequences.

Prescription drug abuse by women appears to be part of a general pattern of malaise and discontent with little or no insight on the part of women using the substances.[20] At one women's counseling center, women requesting general psychological counseling were found to have very high rates of substance abuse—50% dependent upon daily prescription drug use, 10% dependent upon daily alcohol use—and the substance abusing women a high percentage of whom were housewives and agorophobics, were seen clinically as more depressed, more passive, and having little insight into the causes of their distress. Few of these women saw their substance abuse as a problem.

Pill use, then, may be the housewives' methadone maintenance: the daily chemical that maintains and satisfies her drug dependence and that enables her to minimally function without too openly questioning her own role conflicts. On an individual level, this is unfortunate; on a political level, it is cause for feminist outrage, as we see large numbers of women "doped" into a passive acceptance of the female condition by physicians too willing to placate women they see as complaining, hysterical patients.

The sequellae of alcohol abuse by women are far better known and more dramatic. Unlike pill abuse, prolonged alcohol abuse is not as stable and has severe physical and usually social conse-

---

*It is known that alcoholic women are at high risk of becoming drug dependent; it is not known whether the relationship is the same in reverse."

quences. We do not know how many hidden female alcoholics remain hidden throughout a lifetime of drinking; we do know, however, that some women appear for either medical or psychological treatment. If anything, the consequences of alcoholism appear to be more severe for women than for men. For example, while women less frequently suffer legal or job-related consequences, the medical effects of alcohol appear *more* severe for women. In addition, fetal alcohol syndrome of course is a major concern for women. Finally, the social stigma surrounding alcohol use and abuse for women is still quite heavy.[13] In fact, the female alcoholic is still seen as sexually promiscuous and personally irresponsible; and husbands leave alcoholic wives far more frequently than do wives leave alcoholic husbands.[25]

In essence, the social consequences and stigma attached to female chemical abuse seem to be in direct relation to the extent to which such substance abuse interferes with the traditional female role. When, in the case of simple pill abuse, the chemical dependency does not seem to greatly impair functioning in this role, society accepts and, in the case of physicians, condones and promotes substance abuse. When, however, as in the case of alcohol abuse, the chemical appears to interfere with the wife/mother role, society punishes the offending woman who dares transgress her boundaries.

IMPLICATIONS FOR TREATMENT

We have seen that, in order to understand the problems of substance-abusing women, one must view those problems in the context of female oppression. Sexism has helped shape the patterns of how and what chemicals women abuse and why they abuse. Sexism has influenced the individual characteristics of substance-abusing women. And sexism influences the consequences and sequellae of alcohol and pill abuse for women. What then, are the implications of this feminist analysis of chemical abuse in women for treatment?

It seems to follow from this analysis that female substance abusers need a feminist, non-sexist approach to counseling. That approach would incorporate two separate tactics. First, feminist counseling would help substance-abusing women lift the depression that results from self-blame by seeing their problems in a more sociopolitical light. Without abdicating personal responsibility of their own lives, female substance abusers would come to understand their problems in a broader social context; this new perspective could help them resolve sex-role conflict and transform self-blame into healthy anger, and then self-pride.

Second, feminist counseling would help women reject the traditional role expectations that helped straight-jacket them in the first place. Rather than attempt to fit themselves into a way of being that is inappropriate and produces conflict, women can be encouraged to find new identities and lifestyles more appropriate to their inner feelings, not their societally-implanted self-expectations. Thus, lesbian substance abusers can be encouraged to live proud gay lifestyles; women unhappy as housewives can be encouraged to seek careers; women with rigid expectations of feminine behavior can be helped to make their values more flexible.

Evidence that this approach can work comes from the author's own clinical experience. As the founder and director of a feminist women's counseling center in New Jersey, the author saw hundreds of women treated in a group and individual therapy format that included "consciousness-raising," or the feminist political interpretation of individual life events, as well as personal problem-solving geared to specific issues. These women were, on the average, poor to working class non-working housewives with children. The author conducted a two-year follow-up study of over four hundred clients in treatment and discovered these results:[20]

(1) Women's substance abuse (50% pill dependent: 10% alcohol dependent) dropped dramatically and significantly:

(2) At the same time, women's lives became much less stereotypical and traditional; clients got divorced and entered careers in statistically significant numbers;

(3) Significant numbers of women underwent a personality transformation as measured by the Spence-Helmreich PAQ, a test of masculine, feminine, or androgynous traits: hyperfeminine clients at entrance to treatment gained in "masculine" traits such as assertiveness and independence to become more androgynous at termination and follow-up. As one woman said, "I feel stronger now and have better self-esteem. I am more assertive and optimistic about myself. I know where I'm going and do not feel as defeated as I once did."[20]

An example of an alcohol abusing woman who benefited from the consciousness-raising (C-R) approach combined with a more traditional Alcoholics Anonymous approach is Debby S. Debby grew up in a poor white family with a psychotic, physically abusive mother. Removed from her parents' home at age twelve, she was shuffled from foster home to foster home during adolescence. She was raped in one home, and shortly afterwards she got married to escape her surroundings. She had a child by age eighteen, and by her early twenties had developed a serious alcohol problem. Abandoned by her husband, her days consisted primarily of watching soap operas and drinking. A second rape combined with alcoholism precipitated a suicide attempt which brought her to our women's center. Debby spent half a year in a "C-R" group as well as receiving individual help from a feminist counselor. In her counseling, she learned how her upbringing and woman's role had brutalized her while at the same time she was encouraged to take full responsibility for changing her current condition. Eventually, she received job training and now holds a civil service position with the government; she joined A.A. and began recovery from alcohol addiction. She has become strong and assertive where she once was passive and resigned. Debby's case illustrates how feminist therapy can be used to augment rather than supplant a more traditional alcohol counseling approach.

If it sounds as though the author is suggesting that women do well to leave their traditional roles as housewives and mothers, that is exactly correct. At this point, there is wealth of evidence.[2,15,16] that points to the fact that the housewife role as structured in twentieth-century America is an inherently demoralizing and psychologically damaging role for most women. It makes therapeutic good sense to point out to women that this role is a "high stress" occupation more likely to lead to depression and other psychological problems if followed as a permanent "career." Obviously, counselors must at all times be open and flexible and not force their own values upon clients, but in our current state of knowledge it makes as much clinical good sense to point out role risks to a housewife as it does to point out the risk of heart attack to a Type A personality. While this approach *sounds* radical, it is in fact solidly backed by evidence, as is a feminist approach in general.

SUMMARY AND CONCLUSIONS

We have seen in this paper that if we look differentially at patterns of chemical abuse of women versus men, several features become apparent. Traditionally, men express stress by becoming "bad" while women become "mad." In the chemical abuse area, women tend to use the more socially acceptable substances and/ or use them in medicinal or secretive ways. Moreover, chemical abuse in women is closely related to depression, which in turn seems closely tied to the oppression of the female role. Thirdly, women are often introduced to chemical abuse through their dependence upon men: upon physicians, in the case of pill abuse, and upon alcoholic husbands for female alcohol abusers.

On an individual level, female substance abusers are more likely to be lesbians or to have experienced early sexual trauma, factors which make it difficult for them to fit into a conventional feminine role. At the same time, they themselves tend to hold extremely stereotypic values. This clash of value and reality tends to produce *role-conflict* and *depression*, common correlates of female substance abuse. And the consequences of female substance abuse appear to be directly related to a woman's inability to perform her traditional role of wife/mother.

In summary, sexism and female oppression seem intimately tied to women's substance abuse. Feminist counseling has been proposed as a logical approach for female substance abusers. One feminist therapy program that used these principles with apparent success has been described. This program appeared to lead to not only reduced drug and alcohol abuse in clients, but also personality and lifestyle changes consonant with a feminist, non-traditional method.

REFERENCES

1. Armor, D., Polich, J. & Stambul, H. *Alcoholism and treatment.* New York: Wiley, 1978.

2. Bernard, J. *Women, wives, and mothers: Values and options.* Chicago: Aldine, 1975.

3. Brecher, E. *Licit and illicit drugs.* Boston: Little, Brown, 1972.

4. Camberwell Council on Alcoholism. *Women and alcohol.* New York: Methuen, 1980.

5. Chambers, C., Inciardi, J., & Siegel, H. *Chemical Coping: A report on legal drug use in the U.S.* New York: Spectrum, 1975.

6. Chesler, P. *Women and madness.* New York: Avon, 1972.

7. Cohen, S. *The substance abuse problems.* New York: Haworth, 1982.

8. Cooperstock, R. Prescribed psychotropics—the upward trend. *Addictions,* 1974, 21: 34-45.

9. Curlee, J., "A Comparison of Male and Female Patients at an Alcohol Treatment Center." *Journal of Psychology,* 1970, Vol 74, pp 239-247.

10. Cuskey, W., Bremkeemar, T., & Siegel, L. Survey of opiate addiction among females in the United States between 1850 and 1970. In Cohen C., Robinson, S., & Smart, R. eds., *Psychotherapy and drug addiction I: Diagnosis and treatment.* New York: MSS Information, 1974, 55-88.

11. Ehrenreich, B., & English, D. *For Her own Good: 150 Years of Experts' Advice to Women.* New York: Anchor Press, 1979.

12. Gomberg, E. Alcoholism and Women. In B. Kissin & B. Begleiter (Eds.). *The Biology of Alcoholism.* Vol. 4. New York: Plenum, 1976.

13. Gomberg, E. Problems with alcohol & other drugs. In Gomberg. E. & Franks. V. *Gender & Disordered Behavior*, New York: Brunner/Mazel, 1979.

14. Gomberg, E. Women and alcoholism, in V. Franks & V. Burtle. Eds., *Women and therapy:* New York: Brunner/ Mazel, 1974.

15. Gove, W. Sex differences in the epidemiology of mental disorder: evidence and explanations. In E. Gomberg & V. Franks, eds., *Gender and Disordered Behavior*. New York: Brunner/Mazel, 1979.

16. Gove, W. & Tudor, J. Adult sex roles and mental illness. *American Journal of Sociology*. 1973, 78, 812-835.

17. Kammeier, S. Alcoholism is the common denominator: More evidence on the male/female question. Hazelton Papers, No.2, Center City, Minn., 1977.

18. Keennes, R. Images of health and illness in Women. *Journal of drug issues*. 1974, 4(3), 264-267.

19. Mellinger, G., Balter, M., Parry, H., Manheimer, D., & Cisin, I. An overview of psychotherapeutic drug use in the United States. *Archives of General Psychiatry*, 1973, 28(6), 769-83.

20. Nichols, M. *Reclaimed Lives: Experiences of Women and Feminist Counseling.* Doctoral dissertation, Columbia University, 1981.

21. Scarf, Maggie. *Unfinished Business: Pressure Points in the Lives of Women.* Garden City, N.Y.: Doubleday, 1980.

22. Streit, F. Study to determine needs of youth for prevention of drug abuse and other problems, *North Essex Drug Abuse Council Paper*, Essex County, New Jersey, 1974.

23. Weissman, M. & Paykel, E. *The Depressed Woman: A Study of Social Relationships.* Chicago, Ill: The University of Chicago Press, 1974.

24. Wilsnack, S. Sex role identity in female alcoholism. *Journal of Abnormal Psychology*, 1973, 82, 253-261.

25. Wilsnack, S. Alcohol abuse and alcoholism in women, in Pattison, E. & Kaufman, E., *Encyclopedic handbook of alcoholism*, New York: Gardner, 1982.

Alcoholism and Sexual Assault:
A Treatment Approach
for Women Exploring Both Issues

Sandra Turner, M.S.W.
Flora Colao, M.S.W.

INTRODUCTION

In the United States there are 10 million alcoholics, anywhere from 30 to 50% of whom are women.[1] We can predict that one out of three women is sexually assaulted at some time in her life.[2] What is the connection between these two statements? Logic as well as the clinical experiences of the authors dictate that these two issues unavoidably overlap.

There have been some studies that explored the possible connection between rape and alcohol abuse in offenders. John Harrison reported on numerous studies which found that anywhere between 13 and 50% of rapists were drinking at the time of the rape, and 35% of the rapists in one study could be classified as alcoholics.[3] There is not enough evidence to point to a causal relationship between rape and alcohol abuse or alcoholism. However, one researcher concludes: ". . . it is more correct to say that persons who are more likely to commit rape (and other types of assaultive behaviors) are also likely to drink alcohol excessively."[4]

Just as we cannot say that alcohol abuse contributes directly to sexual assault, a causal relationship between women with histories of incest or rape becoming alcoholics has not been shown. However, there does appear to be some relationship between the presence of alcohol abuse in families where incest occurs and the children in these families continuing their connection with alcohol, either becoming alcoholics themselves or marrying alcoholics.

Claudia Black in a survey of 200 adult children of alcoholics found that 30% of the women reported incestuous relationships, 33% were alcoholics themselves, and 35% married alcoholics.

Eighty percent had some difficulty in letting others know what they need or want.[5]

The alcoholic family system is very similar to the incestuous family system in that everyone is protecting a family secret (the incest or the alcoholism). Often there is a fear that if the secret gets out or is publically acknowledged, the family will break up. Some studies have shown the low self-esteem or poor sense of self-worth of women alcoholics.[6] Similarly, in adult survivors of incest, we find that one's sense of self-esteem or self-worth has been damaged. Again it is not possible to predict that incest survivors who are not helped will go on to become alcoholics, but in the family system there are some similar dynamics and some families manifest both problems.

Margaret Hindman found that "children who are physically abused by their parents are at a high risk for turning to alcohol and drug abuse as they grow older."[7] She quoted Dr. Judianne Densen-Gerber's finding that in her residential treatment program for alcoholism and drug abuse, 44% had been sexually assaulted by a father or relative. Kate Rist reports her findings of outcomes for daughters of incest which include: (1) sexual promiscuity coupled with substance abuse, (2) becoming inorgasmic, and (3) later neurotic reactions.[8]

The April, 1983, issue of the "NIAAA Information and Feature Service" reports on a 3-year study done by the Women's Center for Alcoholism Treatment in Phoenix, Arizona. This study found that 63% of their patients reported they had been victims of rape or incest before the age of 14.[9]

Professionals are seldom aware that many women are confronting *both* these issues. Because of the high degree of specialization in the fields of alcoholism and sexual assault, professionals fail to explore the possibility of a connection or that clients may be confronting both issues. The problem of lack of recognition is greater for therapists and counselors who are not sufficiently aware of, or comfortable with, the issue outside their "specialization." Actually, many therapists are not skilled or trained in recognizing either alcohol-related problems or sexual assault-related issues in their female clients.

For the past seven years, St. Vincent's Hospital and Medical Center of New York has had a comprehensive alcoholism treatment program and a rape crisis program. Both are community-based, innovative programs in these fields where the knowledge base is still being developed. The authors have been working together to join their respective areas of expertise and to further explore the relationship between these two issues.

It has only been in the past ten years that there has been any significant clinical research done on the subject of women alcoholics and on the incidence and impact of sexual assault. The possible connection between alcoholism and sexual abuse has not been explored. In addition, professionals and lay people still experience tremendous discomfort with these subjects.

This paper is a report of work within a group setting helping women who need to explore the connection between assault and alcohol abuse in their own lives.

HISTORY

In July, 1978, the Rape Crisis Program presented a workshop on rape for women aftercare patients in the Alcoholism Service. Participants included both women alcoholics and women who had a history of involvement with alcoholics. The workshop provoked feelings of anxiety and discomfort for both the patients and staff involved. For six months, patients who had attended raised issues that seemed to have been aroused by the workshop.

In 1979, the staff on the Rape Crisis Program was invited to provide a series of inservice training sessions to the alcoholism staff on sexual assault. The staff from the Alcoholism Service also provided training sessions for the Rape Crisis Program on recognizing signs and symptoms of alcoholism. The members of both staffs found it difficult to face these issues simultaneously. The primary difficulties seemed to be reluctance to accept the possibility of a connection between these two issues and dismay that clients may need help with both problems. Having to work with a client on an "additional" trauma was sometimes overwhelming for the professional counselor or therapist.

Following this inservice training exchange, staffs from the two programs began referring more clients to each other. For seven months clients who were dealing with both these problems were being treated simultaneously by the two programs. That is they were working on the alcoholism issues with staff from the Alcoholism Service and the sexual assault issues with staff from the Rape Crisis Program.

In June, 1980, the authors initiated a workshop series to provide a forum for women to discuss the connections in their lives between alcoholism and sexual abuse. Participants included women who were actively drinking and alcoholic women who, in recovery, were unblocking past experiences of sexual assault. The format was a supportive education discussion group. It was open to women from both programs.

The authors planned to begin with a series of four workshops and, at the end of the series, evaluate the need for an ongoing group. By the end of the second workshop, it became clear that the intensity of the feelings of the women participants and their tremendous need for support from each other warranted the formation of an ongoing group.

EVOLUTION OF STRUCTURE OF THE GROUP

The original structure for this group was a fluid one. There were initially five women in the group. Because it was a somewhat experimental group, the authors asked the members to define for themselves the initial goals and structure. Most of the women said they wanted a safe place to talk about the sexual abuse they had suffered. Some members came consistently every week, but most felt the need to leave the group periodically for several sessions. This seemed to occur either at a point when they were getting too close to the other members in the group, or when they were not ready to confront or deal with the issues that were being brought up. For example, when many members were getting in touch with their intense anger at their mothers, two women took a leave for several weeks. This presented a difficult adjustment for the group leaders, but it seemed to work very well for the members, who accepted this fluid structure and found it safe and supportive. As one of the members said, "When I need to I come later or don't come at all and no one will hassle me when I come back. I've never had a group like this." This fluid structure had its drawbacks. The main one was that at any given meeting (with the exception of 2-3 core people), there were members who had not been there the previous week. This was sometimes difficult for people who came consistently because they had the fear that something they said drove someone else away. Also it interfered with the group process, because crucial interactions needed to be readdressed or explained.

While "taking a leave" from the group was often used as a safety valve for members to combat feeling too vulnerable or exposed, other members who stayed then felt abandoned. The group also lapsed into a pattern of starting late which became increasingly detrimental to the process. This final factor clarified the fact that it was no longer possible to continue with the fluid structure. After a year, these very serious drawbacks were reviewed and a more formal structure was developed.

CURRENT STRUCTURE OF GROUP

Since the structure of the group had been that of an ongoing therapy group with stated rules and norms, the group members agreed on the need for guidelines. They also acknowledged the need for some assurances of group behavior. This came about as leaders encouraged members to re-evaluate the fluid group structure and discuss to what extent it was or was not meeting their needs.

It was decided that the group would start on time and three unexplained absences would necessitate a group review of the person's status. It was also decided that at approximately two-month intervals a session would be devoted to discussion of group members' goals and other feelings about their own progress.

ISSUES AND STAGES IN THE GROUP PROCESS

Disclosure

Group members spent the first sessions admitting to each other that they had been sexually assaulted. This was done in a casual, off-hand manner, with little or no discussion of their feelings or the impact this had had on their lives. An immediate, very intense bond was formed. For many of the women, this was the first time they had shared this information. The authors noted that this process of disclosure of sexual abuse was similar to what happens in a beginning alcoholism group when people openly state that they are alcoholics and begin to share some of their histories of alcohol abuse. They also experience a great relief and acceptance when they hear other people talk about their own alcoholism. The secret is out at last and the stigma, because it is shared, is reduced.

Some were unable to move beyond this initial level of intimacy established on the basis of similar experience. This will be discussed in greater detail later. Further disclosure beyond this initial reporting of what happened seemed to be very difficult. For many women, it took months for them to be able to look at and talk about the impact of the sexual assaults. Most eventually were able to begin to understand how being sexually assaulted affected other aspects of their lives. Some felt that they increased drinking in order to escape the painful feelings associated with the sexual assault.

Betrayal

Following one disclosure period, the problem those who had been incestuously assaulted faced was the feeling that they were betraying their families by talking about it. Once they began exploring this "betrayal" of their families, they had to confront the reality that their families had betrayed them. Many remembered that as children they didn't tell their mothers what was happening for fear of destroying the family. Later when they did tell, their mothers failed to intervene on their behalves, held them responsible, or didn't believe them. Consequently, in addition to feeling betrayed by the perpetrator, they also felt betrayed by their mothers for not protecting them.

Many of the women who were abused as adults also related to this issue of betrayal because of their families' inappropriate and non-supportive reactions to the sexual assault. For example, one woman recalled coming home with bruises and torn clothing. Her mother reacted by focusing on cleaning her up which added to her feelings of being dirty. She had no recollection of her mother asking her what happened to her or offering comfort. In another case, a woman recalled her father witnessing someone attempting to rape her. He did not try to stop it, and when she was able to successfully get away, he accused her of causing the attack by the way she was dressed. According to the group members, betrayal was one of the most pervasive issues that sexual assault victims had to deal with. This feeling seemed to intertwine around almost every other issue with which they were coping. They often either felt betrayed or that they were betraying someone else.

The authors have observed that betrayal is also an issue faced by women alcoholics. Alcoholism itself is experienced as a betrayal. A woman alcoholic often feels betrayed by her own body and mind. She in good faith intends to control her drinking and cannot understand why she is unable to.

Denial and Closeness

Alcoholics often come from families where one or both parents is an alcoholic. Children and adolescents feel the shame of their family secret of alcoholism and try to protect the family by denying it. Denial is also what the active alcoholic engages in in order to rationalize continued drinking.

Because of the constant preoccupation with betrayal, closeness becomes too great a risk. This has been seen in the group continuously. After a session with considerable disclosure and sharing, many members did not return or if they did were very well defended the following week. Some people even stopped attending the group for several sessions. When members tried to establish relationships with each other outside the group, they were unable to sustain them. There seemed to be a need for the structure of the group to be able to tolerate the feelings of closeness with others.

Trust

The issue that seemed most interwoven with closeness and betrayal was the issue of trust. There had been constant uncertainty about who could be trusted and under what circumstances. The scars of having been betrayed by people they loved came to light as they were encouraged by the leaders to discuss their current relationships. The younger they were at the time of the victimization and betrayal, the greater the difficulty they seem to have in being able to establish trusting relationships. Group members were able to explore their difficulty in trusting people outside the group, but resisted discussing their problems trusting each other.

Because of the early betrayals, these women learned to expect to be hurt or betrayed by people they cared about. In exploring the issue further in the group, many women recognized that they continuously established relationships that were destructive and in which they continued to feel betrayed. For many, this exploration made it possible for the first time to connect their early experience of betayal with their adult patterns of relationships. Consequently, they confronted feelings of loss in regard to what their lives could have been if they had not been victimized. Many shared fantasies of what the possibilities would have been for them had they not been sexually assaulted or had they not been born into families where alcoholism was a problem. The incest survivors focused on such losses more. Because they were usually younger when the sexual assault occurred, and in most cases did not receive validation or any positive intervention on their behalves, they remain more deeply scarred. Group members expressed the feeling that they had lost their childhoods "from that moment on." As soon as they no longer felt protected, they assumed responsibility for keeping the family together. Among the women who were raped as adults, the incident was a trauma to their intimate relationships. Many women reported difficulty having or enjoying sex for several months after being raped. Often husbands or significant others felt overly protective; that their partners had been damaged; or were hesitant to initiate sex out of fear of traumatizing her. These women felt that their ability to trust the motives and intentions of others was affected. Although this was not felt as deeply as it was for those women who had been victims of incest.

Children of alcoholics have difficulty trusting other people because often their experience growing up is that sometimes they can trust and count on their alcoholic parent and sometimes they cannot. They don't understand how their parents can be drunk and untrustworthy one day and sober the next. Children will often try to control their parent's drinking by changing their own behavior and have difficulty understanding why this doesn't work.

Self-Esteem

Because sexual assault pervades so many aspects of the survivor's life (and is still denied as a widespread phenomenon), it has to affect each woman's self-esteem.

For the incest survivor, the answer to the question, "Why did this happen to me?" is an internalized sense of badness or wickedness. Many women have said that the only explanation that made sense to them is that they "must have done something to cause this." The women assaulted in adulthood have the additional burden of feeling that they used poor judgment (or have poor judgment). These feelings of culpability unfortunately are confirmed by our society which blames victims for crimes perpetrated against them. Obviously, feelings of guilt and shame must be dealt with before any genuine anger can be felt. The woman alcoholic also has a very low sense of self-esteem. Our society makes it disgraceful for a wife and mother to be an alcoholic. Women alcoholics accept this stigma and consequently feel a tremendous sense of guilt and shame.

Living with a sense of responsibility for what happened to them left group members with such low self-esteem that they were extremely vulnerable to any criticism or challenge of their behaviors and actions. This left them in an emotionally fragile position. They tended to absorb responsibility for anything that went wrong in their lives. (It is interesting to note that the deeply religious people felt that the abuse was a punishment from God for whatever sins that they had committed or that they had been chosen by God to endure this test of faith. Both attitudes, although possibly consoling as ways of "explaining" the victimization, reinforce the woman's passivity and recurrent victimization.)

Group members reported feeling a tremendous sense of shame. Some felt that the abuse happened to them because they were bad and others felt that the experience made them bad. To illustrate, one woman talked about what an awful child she was and how she felt that her father abused her because of this. Another woman who was raped as a young adult felt that the rape transformed her into a bad person.

Their sense of shame and disgust for what happened to them compelled them to maintain the secret. Both women reported feeling unable to share their experience for fear of repulsing and shocking others.

Anger

It has been surprising to the authors that the only anger ever raised by the women about the assault itself was anger at their mothers for not protecting them. At different times group members also expressed anger (often indirectly) at leaders for not understanding or protecting them from other members or the outside world. They had been unable to get in touch with or express feelings of anger at the perpetrators.

In the authors' experience, this inability to express anger is true for both rape and incest survivors, however, there are somewhat different dynamics involved. The incest survivor fears that getting angry at the perpetrator would cause him to abandon her. She is afraid that the whole family would disintegrate. The rape survivor internalizes society's myths that it is her fault, which prevents her from getting angry and making the rapist responsible. On a deeper level, her unconscious rage feels so overpowering that she fears it could cause her to lose control and become destructive herself. She fears she could have the same power to destroy that the rapist had. In both situations, survivors attempt to deny that the assailant has had such incredible power over their lives by controlling their feelings. Because of these fears, anger is usually repressed or avoided. Anger is a crucial issue for alcoholics. Many people have learned to express their anger only when they are drinking and literally do not know how to do it when sober. Many alcoholic women have to be taught how to express anger—either through assertiveness training, role modeling, supportive provoking, etc.

In the group, when anger began to surface, several members did not return for a session or two; others discussed other things, but not the issues concerning them; some developed physical symptoms, became easily distracted by outside noises, or withdrew. However, the most serious manifestation of their difficulty expressing anger occurred when two of the original members of the group stopped coming for a while and seriously considered quitting the group rather than confront two new members who were provoking a lot of hostility. The authors observed that this carried over into their more intimate personal relationships. To express anger at a friend, lover, or spouse was too great a risk for them to take. Again, carrying their burdens of guilt and shame in addition to repressed anger and fear of their own anger inevitably led many of the women into relationships that were destructive and hurtful to them. This in turn reinforced their conviction that they "don't deserve any better."

THE ROLES AS CO-LEADERS

The roles of the leaders have evolved from knowledgeable, supportive peer facilitators to more objective therapists who help the group establish priorities and focus. As the group format changed from a short-term educational, supportive discussion group to an ongoing therapy group, the consistent members began to form ties with each other and transference issues began to emerge. It was at this time that the leaders began to transform their roles.

This transformation required dealing with feelings about the group as well as counter-transference issues. Members were dealing with competition and rivalry among each other, thereby forcing the leaders to take on a role not originally anticipated. It was necessary to interpret and clarify the sibling-like competitive issues. This required assuming a more observational and directive role. It also caused a state of confusion and frustration among group members during this time of change.

There were new members coming in and some people left. Because of the changing membership, the fluid structure of a support group was maintained. However, once the group established a consistent attendance, it became impossible not to deal with the ongoing therapeutic issues.

This became clear as the authors sensed the magnitude of the anger in the group directed at them. Members were angry that the authors had not taken more control over the group process. They didn't feel safe and wanted protection from each other. The authors become more directive and openly discussed the group's transformation and their responsibility in it. It was very valuable for group members and a sign of their growth to be able to express their resentment toward the authors and to see that their concerns could be responded to. At this point, several clarifying and goal setting sessions were held. In addition, rules about time and behavior were set. Members of the group were relieved by this clarification and by the authors' assumption of more leadership responsibility.

REACTIONS OF COLLEAGUES

One of the most fascinating aspects of this work has been the reactions of other professionals when the authors present the need for sensitivity, to both alcohol abuse and sexual abuse in the treatment of women. Initially there is a denial of the importance of dealing with both issues. Often, those working in the alcoholism field seem to feel that the "real problem" is the alcoholism while those working with sexual assault victims focus on the sexual assault as the "real problem."

For workers in both fields there seems to be a reluctance to deal with the treatment needs of clients coping with the two issues simultaneously. Sometimes this takes the guise of protecting the client from being overwhelmed. For example, an alcoholism counselor stated, "It'll be too much for her to start dealing with the incest now." The rape crisis counselor made the following statement about the same client, "She won't be able to deal with the alcoholism while she's trying to confront the incest; it's too much." The client in this situation specifically stated to both workers that felt she needed to deal with the issues simultaneously as she felt they were completely intertwined.

Many professionals in both fields find themselves overwhelmed because they have to begin dealing with a whole array of unexpected feelings. Their previous acceptance of societal myths in regard to the unfamiliar issue is challenged. For example, one alcoholism counselor found it too frightening to hear the statistics regarding how often rape occurs while a rape crisis counselor was equally shocked upon learning the statistical incidence of alcoholism. In addition, several alcoholism counselors reported unblocking sexual assaults from their pasts, and several rape crisis counselors found themselves no longer able to deny alcoholism in their families or among their friends.

One of the most frequent feelings continually identified by workers in both fields is anger. There are many aspects of both issues that provoke angry feelings. Some feel angry at society for allowing both problems to flourish; others feel angry at victims for raising so many complicated feelings; and many lament the lack of adequate resources and information available. Most state they find themselves feeling uncomfortable when trying to learn about the other issue. It is interesting to note that after workshops and seminars, many professionals express feelings of inadequacy. "I know I'll do or say the wrong thing" is a common statement. The authors feel that this is related to the specification in both fields, and the fact that neither area is given adequate consideration or training. Few professionals in either field are accustomed to giving another problem equal weight. In addition, workers in either one of these areas already feel they are taking on the burden of a secret societal illness; learning about another relatively hidden social problem; and facing the fact that this may be an additional source of suffering in your clients' lives is very painful.

CONCLUSION AND RECOMMENDATIONS

Based on the experience of founding this group and the changing roles as leaders from facilitators to therapists, the authors have a number of recommendations for professionals. First, both fields must develop an awareness of the importance of the other field and of ways in which alcohol abuse and sexual abuse may overlap as treatment issues. Careful histories must be taken and should include questions regarding both issues. Such questions will enable clients to disclose initially or to feel free to come back to the issue at a later date. Of course, education about each issue is crucial, in order for the right program to be chosen and so clients can explore the overlaps and intertwinings of both problems in their lives.

Secondly, there is a need for similar groups. Professionals deciding to develop a similar group program should find co-leaders from the other field, clarify whether the contract will be for a short-term support group or an ongoing therapy group, develop a screening process for group members, and arrange for an outside supervisor. Hopefully, by utilizing these suggestions, some of the problems described above can be minimized.

REFERENCE NOTES

1. *The New York Times.* August 14, 1984, pg. C 3.

2. F. Colao and M. Hunt. "Therapists Coping with Sexual Assault." *Women and Therapy.* Vol. 2, Nos. 2/3. Summer/Fall, 1983, pp. 205-214.

3. W.J. Harrison. "Rape and Alcohol Abuse: Is There a Connection?" *Alcohol Health and Research World.* Spring, 1978, pp. 34-37.

4. J.W. Smith. "Commentary." *Medical Aspects of Human Sexuality,* Vol. 9, No. 3, 1975, pp. 60-65.

5. C. Black. "Children of Alcoholics." *U.S. Journal of Drug and Alcohol Dependence.* March, 1981.

6. L. Beckman. "Self Esteem of Women Alcoholics." *Journal of Studies on Alcohol,* Vol. 39, 1978, pp. 491-498.

7. M. Hindman. "Child Abuse and Neglect: The Alcohol Connection," *Alcohol Health and Research World.* Spring, 1977, pp. 2-7.

8. K. Rist. "Incest: Theoretical and Clinical View." *American Journal Orthopsychiatry,* Vol. 49, 1979, pp. 704-708.

9. U.S. Department of Health and Human Services. "NIAAA Information and Feature Service." No. 106, April, 1983, p. 2.

RECOMMENDED READINGS

Katherine Brady. *Father's Days.* New York: Dell, 1980.

Flora Colao and Tamar Hosansky. *Your Children Should Know.* New York: Bobbs Merrill, 1983.

Judith Herman. *Father/Daughter Incest.* Boston, Mass.: Harvard Univ. Press, 1982

Suzanne Sgroi. *Handbook of Clinical Intervention in Child Sexual Abuse.* New York: Lexington Books, 1982.

Offspring With Fetal Alcohol Effects: Identification and Intervention

Meryl Nadel, M.S.W.

ABSTRACT. Fetal Alcohol Syndrome (F.A.S.) and related defects result from maternal alcohol use during pregnancy and constitute the most common known teratogenic cause of mental deficiency. The three principal features of the syndrome are central nervous system dysfunction, growth deficiency, and craniofacial abnormalities. Many unresolved issues remain. All drinking women of child-bearing age should be screened. Identification and intervention with affected offspring and their parents are essential. Techniques for communicating with the developmentally disabled may be helpful. Prevention efforts are occurring on several fronts.

Alcohol use during pregnancy can result in a variety of congenital abnormalities in the offspring. These defects are called Fetal Alcohol Effects (F.A.E.) or Possible Fetal Alcohol Effects when the abnormalities are limited. The term Fetal Alcohol Syndrome (F.A.S.) is reserved for cases in which the damage is more widespread. F.A.S. is the third most common etiology of congenital mental retardation, exceeded only by Down's Syndrome and Spina Bifida. It is, therefore, the most common teratogenic cause of mental deficiency.

It is essential that those working in the field of alcohol problems become familiar with the effects alcohol can have on the fetus. Such professionals are in a position both to help prevent future cases as well as to identify and refer for treatment those already affected by maternal alcohol intake.

This paper will first provide an overview of Fetal Alcohol Effects and Fetal Alcohol Syndrome. Next, it will focus on the family and offspring: identifying and intervening with those affected by these problems. The concluding section will deal with prevention. When

The author acknowledges helpful suggestions from Muriel Frischer, Ph.D., relating to intervention with offspring.

referring to problems of all those affected by maternal drinking during pregnancy, the term fetal alcohol effects will be used.

OVERVIEW OF FETAL ALCOHOL EFFECTS
AND FETAL ALCOHOL SYNDROME

Fetal alcohol effects have been reported anecdotally for many years. Aristotle as well as writers during the 18th and 19th centuries referred to abnormalities in the children of alcoholic mothers. Sullivan, in 1899, reported a study of over one hundred "female inebriates" and their children.[1] These descriptions and related reports, however, were largely ignored by the scientific community. In 1968 a French study reported on 127 children of alcoholics[2] but even this study received little notice until the first American research was published in the early 1970s. These case reports from the University of Washington[3,4] began to define Fetal Alcohol Syndrome. They were followed by numerous case reports from around the world and, later, by more sophisticated human and animal research.

Examination of affected offspring revealed numerous abnormalities. However, three principal features and a number of associated features have emerged. The following descriptions are summarized from Clarren and Smith[5] to whom the reader is referred for more detailed information.

Central nervous system (C.N.S.) dysfunction is one of these principal features, with mental retardation being a common aspect. A broad range of intelligence is found, but rarely do these patients test at average or better ability. Intelligence is usually lower among patients with more problems in the other areas to be described. Other C.N.S. problems seen in more than half the patients with F.A.S. include poor coordination and muscle tone, irritability in infancy and hyperactivity in childhood. A high incidence of speech and language abnormalities has been described by one group.[6]

A second principal feature is that of growth deficiency, both pre- and postnatally. F.A.S. offspring are born lighter and shorter than average and have a smaller head circumference. They remain below average for their age, over time. They also have less adipose (fat) tissue.

Craniofacial abnormalities constitute the third major feature, making those affected resemble each other more than their own (unaffected) siblings. These include microcephaly, short eye openings, thin upper lip, small or absent philtrum (the vertical groove between the nose and lip), flattened midface, and short, upturned nose.

What have been called associated anomalies include a variety of features found in 50% or less of the observed cases. Some of these problems are heart murmurs, posterior rotation of the ears, unusual palmar creases, and malformations of the eyelids and mouth. These anomalies together with the craniofacial characteristics mentioned have been referred to as the dysmorphic features of F.A.S.[7]

As alluded to above, a diagnosis of F.A.S. is made when problems exist in all three principal areas while F.A.E. indicates problems in two of the principal areas coupled with maternal drinking during pregnancy. The term "Possible Fetal Alcohol Effects" is used when signs are found which are "compatible with, but not diagnostic of alcohol-related damage. . . ."[8]

As would be expected in an area so recently opened to scientific investigation, estimates of frequency of fetal alcohol effects vary and continue to be revised and updated. Frequencies for F.A.S. of 1 in 1000 to 1 in 2425 births and for fetal alcohol effects of 3-5 births per 1000 have been suggested.[5,9] However, it is possible that many cases where the abnormalities are subtle or confined to one system are not identified as being related to alcohol use.

There appears to be a dose-response curve for fetal alcohol effects. In other words, the more a pregnant woman drinks, the more likely she will give birth to a baby with fetal alcohol effects. Similarly, the affected offspring is more likely to be further over on the continuum of effects with a more heavily drinking mother. In alcohol-abusing women, as many as one half have adverse perinatal outcomes of some sort.[10] According to Ashley, only chronically alcoholic women have given birth to offspring with "fullblown" F.A.S.[11]

Findings concerning fetal alcohol effects among offspring of moderate and "social" drinkers are less clearcut (definitions often used are: heavy drinking = six or more drinks per day, moderate or "social" drinking = an average of two drinks per day). Several studies have found significantly lowered birthweights in the offspring of women who drank moderately in either the very beginning or the second half of pregnancy.[12,13] Although these and other studies suggest fetal effects related to moderate drinking, Sokol states, in a recent paper, that findings in this area are inconclusive.[9] However, it is important to note that neither a "safe" level of drinking during pregnancy nor a threshhold level for fetal alcohol effects has been documented.

Timing of exposure of the fetus to alcohol and pattern of drinking in relation to the type and extent of damage produced are other areas in which research is in the early stages. It is conceivable that a one-time binge at a crucial time in the fetus' development may cause different or greater damage than daily drinking. Similarly, heavy daily drinking at one point during pregnancy may cause little damage while more moderate drinking at another point could cause considerable damage. Genetic predisposition is another variable.

Although knowledge in the area remains limited, the U.S. Surgeon General advises abstinence during the entire pregnancy.[14]

WHO ARE THE MOTHERS?

Who are these women? Where can they be found? Like other people with alcohol problems, they transcend social, economic, ethnic, and racial categories. Those at greatest risk, the chronic alcoholics, include women easily spotted: in and out of treatment programs, disaffiliated, unemployed. However, they are also the upper-middle class homemaker with several "normal" children, the career woman, the "swinging single." Another group which includes heavy drinkers are adolescents, also at high risk for unplanned pregnancies. "Situational alcoholism," increased drinking in response to a particular stress, should not be overlooked in a person not identified as alcoholic. Since safe limits have not been established; the daily beer, wine, or cocktail drinker, the weekend partier, the occasional binger, and even the infrequent drinker should all be identified when they are contemplating pregnancy or have become pregnant.

A brief but specific drinking history should be taken to assess the attitudes, behavior, and knowledge regarding alcohol in women of childbearing age. If alcohol *use* is discovered, education regarding drinking and pregnancy can be provided. If alcohol abuse seems evident, appropriate intervention should take place immediately.

Suggestions for taking a drinking history are contained in an article by Sokol and Miller.[15] They propose a sequence of questions beginning with fairly non-threatening ones ("Has anyone in your family ever had a drinking problem?" "Do you ever drink . . . ?" "When did you first start drinking?"), leading to questions regarding early drinking practices, to current use, and finally, to circumstances, pattern, and effects of current abuse, when indicated. Standardized drinking questionnaires may also be employed.

An approach with the pregnant woman is to ask whether a change in her drinking habits has occurred since pregnancy. (A decrease in drinking occurs spontaneously in many women.) The response provides an opening for further questions regarding amounts, pattern, etc.

In summary, drinking during pregnancy carries a risk to the offspring such that all drinking women of childbearing age should be identified, educated, and offered treatment when the latter is indicated.

IDENTIFICATION OF AFFECTED OFFSPRING

Diagnosis of fetal alcohol effects is complex and requires specialized clinical skills. This section is not meant to provide such skills but, rather, to describe physical and psychological markers which should lead the clinician to suspect fetal alcohol effects, gather some additional information, and refer the person for further evaluation. This evaluation would include medical and psychological examinations. The recently published *Manual for the Assessment of Fetal Alcohol Effects*[7] might be employed as an aid in the assessment. In some medical centers there are physicians who have begun to act as referral resources for these evaluations.

Those with fetal alcohol effects may be of all ages. Although specific intervention with the child with fetal alcohol effects would probably be more extensive than that with the adult, the knowledge that the latter is affected would lead the clinician to provide more appropriate treatment for that person while dealing with the current social functioning problem.

It must be re-emphasized that there is a continuum of fetal alcohol effects such that precisely the same combination of features does not reappear. In some cases appearance may be more striking while in others behavioral problems or intellectual impairment may predominate. In milder cases, the effects may be subtler. The article by Clarren and Smith[5] delineates frequencies. Abnormalities which the non-physician might observe generally fall into the categories of appearance, behavior, cognitive deficits, and personality.

The physical characteristics of a person with fetal alcohol effects nearly always include small size, specifically, low height and weight and small head circumference. As noted, facial features make these patients, particularly as small children, resemble each other. They appear to have a very long, flat space between nose and upper lip. The flattened philtrum and short, upturned nose are responsible for giving this impression. The middle of the face is also frequently flat in appearance. The eyes are small and the upper lip is unusually thin. The jaw appears small in young children but may appear disproportionally large in adolescents, having grown more than the rest of the face.

The infant with fetal alcohol effects is irritable and fretful. There are major sleep disturbances, weak suck, and other feeding difficulties. Such babies do not habituate readily to new stimuli. As they grow older, these children are hyperactive and uncoordinated (problems with both fine and gross motor control).

Cognitively, the average IQ of F.A.S. children is about 60-75 (mildly retarded).[16] IQ tends to remain stable over time and is unrelated to whether the person was raised in the alcoholic family or in a non-alcoholic situation (foster or adoptive home, living with father, mother recovered, etc.)[17] Apparently, the damage done prenatally is permanent. Poor attentional skills and problem-solving abilities have also been noted.[18]

When it is mentioned, most offspring with fetal alcohol effects are described as being sociable and personable.

Two recent reports illustrate the variability of the syndrome. In a study of children referred to a learning disorders unit, Shaywitz, Cohen, and Shaywitz[19] describe a group of fifteen subjects whose mothers drank heavily during pregnancy. Although these children had fetal alcohol effects including small size, fine motor dysfunction, and typical facial dysmorphology; their IQ scores ranged from 82-113 with a mean of 98.2. Thus, they would be considered average rather than intellectually retarded. Their main problem was school failure and virtually all were considered hyperactive.

Another report from the same center[20] describes two offspring of drinking mothers. These boys had rather *large* head circumference, normal size and growth, and facial features typical of fetal alcohol effects, and severe C.N.S. dysfunction. The latter included hyperactivity, distractability, auditory hypervigilence, poor sound discrimination, and language and cognitive problems. Both were developmentally delayed in language acquisition and unable to use language appropriately. Cognitively, there was a thought disorder and underlying conceptual confusion. They were disinterested, anxious, and confused in social situations. Interestingly, both boys tested in the borderline retarded range on verbal intelligence tests but average or above on nonverbal intelligence tests.

Many questions remain unanswered. Retrospective human studies provide inaccurate data, since they depend on the mother's recollection of her drinking pattern over a nine-month timespan. Prospective studies are expensive and may present ethical problems. Clearly, however, since the range and number of potential problems is so great, any clinician working with the offspring of alcoholic women should be conscious of the possibility of fetal alcohol effects in this population.

INTERVENTION WITH THE FAMILY

When an infant or older child has been identified as having fetal alcohol effects, sensitive and early intervention with the entire family is indicated. The recognition that alcohol use could be a problem is crucial to helping the family. Of prime importance for the clinician is the fact that the mother may never have considered herself a person with an alcohol problem. The notion that she could be an alcoholic or that she needs treatment may be a new one for her.

Thus, the professionals' (Wright suggests a team of at least physician and social worker[21]) first task is to present objectively the facts connecting the baby's abnormalities with the mother's use of alcohol. If it was not done earlier, a drinking history will help define the nature of the alcohol use. As the drinking history is being obtained, the worker will begin to sense the role of denial in the maintenance of the drinking. If the client is evasive, highly defensive, and angry about the information being sought, the rest of the family might be involved to further assess the situation. It may then be helpful to meet with the entire family for a session in which the alcoholic is confronted by those affected by her drinking. This approach is widely used. It has been the author's experience that such an intervention, when done with support and concern, can help the patient acknowledge an alcohol problem.

If the mother acknowledges and accepts the idea that alcohol is a problem for her and has caused damage to her offspring, she may be overwhelmed by feelings of guilt and depression. Such a reaction is realistic and healthier than denial. In the short term, the mother needs support and acceptance by the professionals helping her. It is beneficial to emphasize that she did not knowingly harm her child and to focus on the present and future once the initial crisis of recognition is over.

A treatment plan for the longer term should focus upon helping the mother deal with her drinking problem, care for her child, and follow through with recommendations for the child's treatment. Although an array of alcoholism treatment resources exists, very few residential services provide facilities so that children may accompany their mothers. Similarly, outpatient facilities generally do not provide childcare while the mother is being seen. Thus, treatment is complicated by the need to find a caretaker for the child if, in fact, placement has not occurred. Such a separation could, in some cases, enable the patient to make better use of treatment than if her attention must be divided between child and treatment program. On the other hand, issues of bonding and separation anxiety must also be considered, depending on the child's age. Regardless of the specific type of treatment, the mother will need much encouragement in this difficult, two-pronged situation. If supportive family members are available, they should be involved.

The mother may also need guidance in caring for her child. Even if the child has no major physical problems, behavioral difficulties and cognitive deficits may exist. To deal patiently with a hyperactive child who sleeps and eats poorly, while recovering from one's own alcoholism is difficult, at best. A home health aide or other support person in the home may be helpful.

Finally, even the most sincere and involved mother may need help in carrying out treatment recommendations for the child. Concrete services, such as transportation assistance, may be necessary to enable the child to make use of programs located far from home.

If the immediate family is intact, the father's involvement should be sought. His initial reaction may well be one of anger at his partner. He should be encouraged to express his feelings and helped to come to terms with the situation, again, with the emphasis that the damage was not knowingly caused. In some situations significant others such as parents may substitute for the spouse.

The importance of treating the mother regardless of who has custody of the child cannot be overemphasized. Being in her childbearing years, she is at risk for giving birth to additional children with fetal alcohol effects, should she continue to drink. If the impact of a diagnosis of fetal alcohol effects serves to penetrate the denial surrounding the alcoholic's drinking, her chances of recovery may be at their zenith.

It should be noted that a child with fetal alcohol effects whose custodial parent(s) is (are) drinking may be at high risk for abuse.

INTERVENTION WITH THE OFFSPRING

It is preferable that diagnostic assessment and specific treatment planning be done by specialists in this area. The affected person will be referred to programs geared to his/her disabilities rather than their etiology. These programs include infant stimulation, therapeutic nurseries, remediation clinics, other special education programs, etc. These programs have counseling staffs to work with family and client, focussing primarily on the client's functioning, not the etiology of his/her disabilities. This is appropriate when the mother's drinking is not a current issue in the offspring's life.

The alcoholism treatment professional may become involved with the affected offspring when the mother enters alcoholism treatment. Now the focus is on helping the alcoholic's son or daughter understand what alcoholism is, how family members are affected, and how each member can be helpful to the entire family. Individual sessions may be necessary to verify this member's comprehension of the situation, answer questions, and provide additional support as needed.

The following guidelines on communication with developmentally and learning disabled people are relevent to working with those with fetal alcohol effects. Statements should be concrete, brief, and specific. Subtleties should be avoided and analogies omitted or simplified. Each session should have limited goals.

As the interview continues, one should acknowledge that you understand the person may have trouble remembering. Visual aids and other devices may help the person focus and ask clarifying questions.

Throughout the interview it is helpful to rephrase your points in various ways and to verify what the person has understood. Asking him/her to repeat what has been said can provide such feedback. A relaxed, unhurried atmosphere is essential in helping the affected child or adult understand the current situation. Once a rapport has been established, the person with fetal alcohol effects can often be integrated into an existing family program. Even if the affected offspring is developmentally or learning disabled, inclusion in family conferences and group sessions may give this person a sense of being an equal member of the family and acknowledge his/her concern.

PREVENTION

Unlike many other birth defects, fetal alcohol effects are completely preventable. By definition, true prevention efforts must take place prior to pregancy. To avoid damage from drinking in the period before pregnancy is recognized, cessation must occur before conception. Thus, education and treatment programs should be aimed at *all* women of childbearing age. This population can be reached both through public education (also important for their significant others) and professional training. Several states and counties (New York State, Wisconsin, King County, Wa.) have embarked upon ambitious efforts of this type, utilizing pamphlets, broadcast media, speakers, newspapers, and bumper stickers to reach the general public. Professionals have been educated through training sessions and information packets. The Pregnancy and Health program in Seattle has also employed a 24-hour crisis telephone line with success.

Another aspect of prevention is intervention in early pregnancy to stop or decrease drinking for the remainder of the pregnancy. When women who drank heavily during their first trimester abstained or reduced their drinking before and during the third trimester, their offspring were born with significantly fewer abnormalities than those continuing heavy drinking throughout pregnancy.[22] In this study 67% of the offspring of the former group were described as normal while only 7% of the latter met these criteria. Thus, intervention can be highly beneficial. The drinker's motivation is enhanced by the knowledge that one's unborn child will benefit from abstinence. As already noted, knowledge about fetal alcohol effects can impact upon the alcoholic's use of denial.

Rosett[23] has proposed a "three-phase classification" of drinking patterns which provides practical guidance for treating the pregnant drinking woman. Social phase drinkers use alcohol to "facilitate socialization" and can stop drinking when informed that heavy drinking could harm the fetus. Symptom-relief phase drinkers are primarily depressed, requiring counseling and assistance with problems they face before they can stop drinking. Women in the syndrome phase are physiologically dependent upon alcohol and require inpatient detoxification and continued treatment. Abortion can also be explored as an alternative, if the pregnancy is not advanced. With these guidelines, treatment planning for the pregnant, drinking woman is fairly straightforward.

In summary, drinking while pregnant can cause a range of problems in the offspring, which can be prevented but must be identified and treated when they occur. In women, education and treatment are appropriate before conception, during pregnancy, and after childbirth. Offspring must be evaluated and treated promptly if fetal alcohol effects are present. Increased awareness on the part of professionals in both the fields of child development and alcoholism is essential to stop this needless damage.

NOTES

1. These and others cited in Rosett, H.L., "Effects of maternal drinking on child development: an introductory review," *Annals N.Y. Acad.Sci. 273:* 115-117, 1976.

2. Lemoine, P., Harousseau, H., Borteyru, J.P., and Menuet, J.C., "Les enfants de parents alcooliques: anomalies observees a propos de 127 cas," *Quest Med 25:* 476-482, 1968.

3. Ulleland, C.N., "The offspring of alcoholic mothers," *Ann. N.Y. Acad.Sci. 197:* 167-169, 1972.

4. Jones, K.L., Smith, D.W., Ulleland, C.N. Streissguth, A.P., "Pattern of malformation in offspring of chronic alcoholic mothers," *Lancet, 1:* 1267-1271, 1973.

5. Clarren, S.K. and Smith D.W., "The Fetal Alcohol Syndrome," *New Eng.J.Med. 298:* 1063-1067, 1978.

6. Iosub, S., Fuchs, M., Bingol, N., and Gromisch, D.S., "Fetal Alcohol Syndrome revisited," *Pediatrics, 68:* 475-479, 1981.

7. Graham, J.M., Phillips, E.L.R., Herman, C.S., Little, R.E., *Manual for the assessment of fetal alcohol effects,* U. of Wash., Seattle, 1982.

8. Ibid., pg. 20.

9. Sokol, R.J., "Alcohol and abnormal outcomes of pregnancy," *Canadian Med.Assn.J. 125:* 143-148, 1981.

10. Sokol, R.J., Miller, S.I., Reed, G., "Alcohol abuse during pregnancy: an epidemiologic study," *Alcoholism 4:* 135-145, 1980.

11. Ashley, M.J., "Alcohol use during pregnancy: a challenge for the '80's," *Canadian Med.Assn.J., 125:* 141-143, 1981.

12. Little, R.E., "Moderate alcohol use during pregnancy and decreased infant birth weight," *Amer. J. of Pub. Hlth., 67:* 1154-1156, 1977.

13. Hanson, J.W., Streissguth, A.P., and Smith D.W., "The effects of moderate alcohol consumption during pregnancy on fetal growth and morphogenesis," *The J. of Pediatrics, 92:* 457-460, 1978.

14. Surgeon General's Advisory on Alcohol and Pregnancy, *FDA Drug Bulletin, 11:* 9-10, 1981.

15. Sokol, R.J. and Miller, S.I., "Identifying the alcohol-abusing obstetric/gynecologic patient: a practical approach." *Alcohol Health and Research World, 4:* 36-40, 1980.

16. Clarren, S.K., "Recognition of fetal alcohol syndrome," *JAMA 245*: 2436-2439, 1981.

17. Streissguth, A.P. Herman, C.S., and Smith, D.W., "Stability of intelligence in the fetal alcohol syndrome: a preliminary report," *Alcoholism 2*: 165-170, 1978.

18. Streissguth, A.P., "Psychologic handicaps in children with fetal alcohol syndrome," *Ann.N.Y.Acad.Sci., 273*: 140-145, 1976.

19. Shaywitz, S.E., Cohen, D.J., and Shaywitz, B.A., "Behavior and learning difficulties in children of normal intelligence born to alcoholic mothers," *J. of Pediatrics 96*: 978-982, 1980.

20. Shaywitz, S.E., Caparulo, B.K., and Hodgson, E.S., "Developmental language disability as a consequence of prenatal exposure to ethanol," *Pediatrics 68*: 850-855, 1981.

21. Wright, J.M., "Fetal alcohol syndrome: the social work connection," *Health and Social Work 6*: 5-10, 1981.

22. Rosett, H.L., Ouellette, E.M., Weiner, L., and Owens, E., "Therapy of heavy drinking during pregnancy," *Obs. and Gynec. 51*: 41-46, 1978.

23. Ibid.

A Supervisory
Group Process Approach
to Address Staff Burnout
and Countertransference
in Alcoholism Treatment

Kathy Stillson, A.C.S.W.
Carole Katz, A.C.S.W.

ABSTRACT. Burnout and countertransference are problems frequently encountered by alcoholism treatment staff. A clinical excerpt from an experimental supervisory group process approach is presented in dialogue form together with the underlying theoretical principles and comments on the interventions of the co-leaders. The group dialogue illustrates a method of mediating these feelings of countertransference and resolving them so the therapist is free to respond creatively to the patient's needs.

This paper begins with an introduction to our concept of countertransference and burnout, with suggestions for their causes and effects. We then give clinical excerpts from our work with an analytic group supervisory process, which is particularly effective in mediating burnout and in enabling participants to make use of induced feelings. The paper concludes with a discussion of the principles of this work. This process is very helpful to people working in the field of alcoholism, for it is often difficult to understand and use our induced feelings to help our clients productively.

DEFINING BURNOUT

Burnout is an issue which has become increasingly discussed in the past few years, both as a general problem in our society and as a problem in the helping professions.[2,4,10] Particular attention has been paid recently to the phenomenon of burnout in alcoholism treatment personnel, which is the focus of this paper.

Burnout has been defined as "a syndrome of physical and mental exhaustion involving the development of a negative self-concept, negative job attitudes, and a loss of concern and feeling for clients."[10]

The best way to assess burnout in oneself and one's supervisees is to be alert to the following questions:

1. Do you suffer from physical complaints: Headaches, pains, colds?
2. Have you lost your sense of humor about yourself and your job?
3. Do you have trouble waking up and dragging yourself to work every day? Does every day begin to feel the same . . . like a treadmill?
4. Do you find yourself "spacing out"—tuning out when you're in session with clients?
5. Do you have trouble relaxing when you get home? Do you feel a need for a drink or a pill?
6. Are the hours you spend with clients becoming the most dreaded of your day?
7. Do you feel like you do all the work and never get any appreciation?
8. Do you find yourself feeling about your patients "They're just a bunch of drunks . . . I can't help them at all. It's a waste of time to try?"

John Wallace traces the development of the stages of burnout as part of the following general stress reaction: It begins with an "alarm state," which is the body's normal reaction to stress. The body's energy and defenses prepare to deal with a threat. However, if the situation doesn't change, frustration arises which leads to the "resistence state." Here, the energy of the person is going directly to dealing with the stress, and the task becomes secondary. This is usually the beginning of burnout. A downward spiral begins, leading to further frustration, feelings of inadequacy, loss of self-esteem and depression. Finally comes the "exhaustion state," when the person's adaptive capacities have broken down. This is a full blown case of burnout.[14]

BURNOUT IN THE HELPING PROFESSIONS

While burnout is found in all fields of work, it is especially prevalent in the helping professions. In other professions, and in business, there are resources to turn to for whatever tasks need to be accomplished. In the human services field, however, the resources we have to use are often within ourselves. Therefore, the risk of depleting these resources is greater, and the need to reclaim them is of such importance.

Additionally, we are feeling the effects of Reaganomics on our work and our lives. The elderly, the "working poor," minority group members as well as the unemployed poor are facing more reality-based problems with fewer resources to help. It will become harder for us to feel helpful and effective as our clients feel more and more impotent and hopeless. In order to turn this "parallel process" around, we need to find cost-effective methods to replenish ourselves and our staffs.

Why people become burned out is a very complex question, involving our personal as well as our professional lives. Most of us come into the helping professions out of a desire to be helpful to others, to have an effect, and to learn about ourselves. Many come with an idealistic sense of what is possible, and we expect to have much more control, immediate success, and appreciation from clients than we actually receive. Our education doesn't prepare us for the real work world that awaits us.[a]

It is the needs within us to be acknowledged, remembered, to be important, which "hook us" and can cause us trouble if we try to get them met by our patients.

Another problem connected with burnout is the difficulty feeling competent when we work under such difficult odds, with an unclear sense of how to define our successes. There is a need for us to relabel what we call a success for an alcoholic, so that we are able to see growth not just from our clients with complete recoveries, but also from our clients who show longer periods of abstinence, whose relapses are shorter and less severe, and who are functioning generally better in their lives.[9]

THE RELATIONSHIP OF BURNOUT
TO COUNTERTRANSFERENCE

Burnout is also related to countertransference. For purposes of this article we shall define countertransference as feelings that are induced in us by our patients. In alcoholism treatment, burnout can manifest itself in many ways which are related to countertransference issues. One process which can happen is when we as therapists feel as if we have caught the disease of our patients. For example, we can take on the characteristics of a chronic alcoholic—impulsivity, low frustration tolerance, helplessness, feelings of emptiness, hoplessness, despair, emotional detachment, impotence, and cynicism. We are also working with people who have a set of characteristics which can be "catching" in an agency. For example, it is common to find one's self or one's staff wanting to respond impulsively to impulsive demands from patients . . . feeling "I must do this right now for this person"—losing a sense of how many crises this person has created for him/herself of the same nature. It is our job to teach the person not to act impulsively, not to increase the dependency, but to help the patient function more independently. It is just at this point that we have the opportunity to turn around and transform the "parallel process," the chain of induced feeling from patient to therapist to supervisor.[3]

Another common response is feelings of hopelessness, passivity, and even feelings of drunkeness. In some situations the entire staff will respond as a system to a set of symptoms that were difficult for them to tolerate, for example, feeling, and acting, in a punitive manner toward patients. This can come about as a result of a jealousy that we experience as therapists. Our patients are acting out their infantile omnipotence insisting that they are in control of their fate and stirring up in us very early infantile material. We have to then struggle to cope with and "control" those feelings in ourselves, and begin to envy our patients who can just act out and "be the baby" . . . so to speak.[13]

Another problem that can happen is feeling a need to save the patient. In the same way the patients often cannot admit to the first step in AA—that of being powerless over controlling alcohol, we refuse to recognize that we cannot control the patient's decisions. If we have these feelings and are not able to recognize them as countertransference, we may find ourselves being resentful, angry, bored, fatigued, helpless or completely numb. If we can identify these feelings and use them to understand our patients, we will be able to regain our energy.

We believe that most therapists know what to do and can act, except when they are caught in countertransference feelings that are preventing them from feeling their creativity and energy. It is our contention that being aware of our induced feelings can provide us with an invaluable resource in understanding and working with our patients. The process involves allowing ourselves to intuit, to listen openly, to grasp the latent content of what our patients are saying and doing and to know ourselves well enough to recognize our own feelings from those that are induced by our patients.

CLINICAL EXCERPTS OF THE GROUP PROCESS

We hope the following case material will further illucidate the relationship between burnout and induced feelings. Although condensed and somewhat simplified, the material will also exemplify the principles of the supervisory group process approach we use to mediate these feelings and help us use them effectively in our work.

The excerpts included are typical of leadership methods and the initial responses of workshop participants to their first introduction to this technique. The example we are using is a group of alcoholism treatment personnel lead by two group leaders (GL). The process works equally well with one group leader.

We began by setting the atmosphere with an initial go-around, encouraging participants to introduce themselves and indicate why they have come and what they hoped to gain. We stressed the commonality of the issues raised. We then discussed the principles already outlined in a handout (see Appendix A), briefly explaining that they are best understood if experienced and asking participants to pay particular attention to the exact words of the presenter.

The next step was to invite participants to share with the group particular problems they were having in their work. Excerpt:

A.   I wanted to talk about this couple I've been working with for the past few years. Everyone in the clinic can't stand them and they always stop me when I want to talk about them in supervision group. They all groan when I mention their names. I'm really

A courageous group participant speaks up. This member was particularly open about his conflicts so that the group process was speeded up. The feelings expressed by A. are indicative of the burnout syndrome. They indicate the kind of dehumanization we begin to feel as therapists, when we begin to unsure what I should do with them. They had this fight and they're both very crazy in addition to being alcoholics—they've both been sober for six months now. This is really the first serious fight they've had since they've been sober. I find myself very anxious. I'm doing a lot of talking and trying to patch things up and keep everybody happy. Such overt hostility—it was scary and they might drive themselves to drink again. It started with her screaming and yelling at him, as usual. Then he threatened to leave her as he usually does. Then he threw all her clothes out the window and threatened to throw her out next. No one at the clinic thinks I should work with them. Maybe they're right. They are hopeless. They were screaming so loud that they disrupted the entire clinic, for a change.

talk about our patients as hopeless.

GL2 Thank you for presenting this case. What I'd like us to do first is for anyone of you who'd like to—to share with us exactly what you heard A. say up to now.

This is done to set the atmosphere and to begin teaching the process of listening to the exact words of the presenter.

R. Have you tried talking this case over with your immediate supervisor?

GL2 That's a good question but before we get into questions, I'd like those of you who feel like it to say what you heard A. saying.

Often questions are asked or suggestions offered rather than reflecting back what the presenter said, making it necessary for the group leader to refocus the discussion.

A period followed with group members asking questions and making suggestions.

S. Before I say what I heard, I'd really like to know if they've had a period of sobriety like this in the past.

It's very difficult for participants to stay with the exact words of the presenter and the feelings they engender. The leader must gently keep refocusing on the needs of the presenter.

GL2 I can hear your need for more information but I wonder if you'd be willing to share with the group the feelings you had that made you ask that question. If you can remember them.

Again the leader refocuses the discussion and stays with the latent content at the same time maintaining a supportive atmosphere.

S. Well, I remember how it makes me feel when I have a patient who's been sober for a period of time and I'm afraid they might get drunk if anything really upsetting happens to them. I get to feeling responsible to keep everything calm.

A sharing of induced feelings by a group member.

A. Yeah, that's really part of it. I know I'm not really responsible for their lives but still I feel it's up to me. They've never been sober before.

The presenter feels understood and responds.

GL1   Would anyone else like to share what you heard?

> In the initial session, when teaching the process, the leader is constantly focusing the group.

E.   What I heard him saying? The first thing I heard him say was that he was in a difficult situation with people he'd worked with for a long time. He sounds like he's afraid of being in the middle, he doesn't want to side with either one of them.

GL1   Is that helpful to you—that feeling of not wanting to take sides.

> The group leader turns to the presenter, who is always the final judge of the accuracy of his or her needs.

A.   Yeah, that's true. It took years to get M (the wife) to trust me and I don't want to lose that trust—but (shrugs)

H.   I just feel how frightened he feels. Such a bad situation.

> More sharing of induced feelings. The group is also learning how to focus.

GL1   Is that helpful to you?

> The presenter is the final judge of the accuracy of his or her needs.

A.   Yeah, because it's so out of control. (pause)

M.   (jumps in) What struck me also is this question of what's appropriate. How can you allow patients to

> The group members have focused on their feelings but are also responding from induced feelings of "out of control," "ur-

disrupt a clinic? What's the role of the therapist?

gency" and jumping into the process rather than letting the speaker finish his or her thoughts.

A.   That's part of it. Their be-
     havior is bizarre — they
     drive everyone away.
     (pause)

C.   (jumps in) I heard a sense
     of urgency too. This had to
     be taken care of immedi-
     ately. The fighting had to
     be stopped.

GL1 A sense of urgency. Does
     that have meaning for you?

The group leader refocuses the discussion to the needs of the presenter.

A.   Yeah, everything in these
     people's lives is urgent and
     I have to urgently make it
     better and I can't and I
     don't know what would.
     (Another hopeless shrug)

This is an example of burnout and induced feelings which re-sult in impulsive behavior. The couple induces the feelings in the therapist and the therapist in the group.

J.   (jumps in) I think you
     should never let them act
     out in the clinic. I don't see
     why administration hasn't
     been brought in to deal
     with that issue.

J. responds to the resulting feelings of frustration by acting impulsively interrupting and blaming the presenter.

GL2 I can see that J. shares your
     feeling of urgency and
     frustration as to how to
     make it better.

This somewhat hostile response is relabeled by the group leader rather than dealt with directly.

Were this an on-going group the leaders would explore this re-sponse as a way to further un-derstand our countertransference feelings in the parallel process.

A.   It's nice to know someone shares my feelings.

GL2 Does anyone else want to share what you heard? (no one else does) I'd like to ask A. how he feels right now. Has this been helpful?

The presenter is the final judge.

A.   Yes, it's been helpful. I feel a little bit better. The things that were said are true but I still don't know what to do.

GL2 I'd like to share what I heard A. say. He began by saying that "no one wants him to talk about this case in group supervision. They all groan when he mentions their names."

Not until all of what the presenter feels has been heard will the presenter feel understood. Therefore, the group leader refocuses again on the initial exact words of the presenter.

M.   (pause) I work with A. and I had no idea how alone he felt with this case. It's true they are very difficult and manage to offend everyone they come in contact with.

A.   Yeah, that's the worst of it (body visibly relaxing) I've been working with them for years. No one wanted to hear about it. They all thought it was hopeless and yet they've been sober for six months. No one cared or knew. I can't do it all myself.

Often signs of feeling understood are nonverbal.

R. I had the same experience
    with a couple I worked
    with. It's the isolation that
    kills you.

S. And to feel so
    unappreciated by
    everyone—the couple, the
    staff. Look at what you've
    done. You helped these
    two people be sober for six
    months.

A. Yeah, that's really it. Be-   Just as our patients have a need
    ing alone and unappreci-   to be understood and appreci-
    ated. I feel much better   ated so do their therapists. The
    (big smile). Better than I   achievement of the "resolution
    have in a long time. (The   experience" is indicated by the
    entire group is now   smiling group and other non-
    smiling.)   verbal cues.

M. Maybe I can help. I'll cer-   Problem solving cannot occur
    tainly support your talking   until the presenter feels under-
    about them in group super-   stood (the "resolution experi-
    vision. Maybe there's a   ence"). Countertransference that
    way you don't have to be   is not understood interferes with
    so alone. Maybe we could   the learning process. The pre-
    get them in a group or get   senter and often other group
    you a co-therapist. They're   members are freed up to ap-
    too much for any therapist   proach their work with new in-
    alone.   sights and renewed energy. The
                                          group can also now move on to
                                          more didactic material.

A. You know, I've been
    thinking about W and M
    (the couple). I know they
    act crazy in a certain way
    but they dress the way they
    do to get attention. They
    don't know how else to do

it. They're so needy . . . I
just thought . . . I'm not
sure why . . . they probably fight the way they do to
get each other's attention.
Now that they've stopped
drinking, they're probably
at odds with what to do
with each other. I could
start to talk with them
about that. It might help
. . . It might be fun to try.

The group continued by
discussing some of the particularly difficult issues in
working with alcoholics:
How unappreciated one
can feel, the sense of urgency, and the induced
feeling of hopelessness.

(The group agreed that this
method was helpful in un-
derstanding the roots of
these issues.) The group
concluded with a discus-
sion of the importance of
listening to the exact words
to understand what was really being presented, as a
first step in learning and
changing.

THE PRINCIPLES OF THE SUPERVISORY GROUP PROCESS APPROACH

The interactional, focused listening, analytic group supervisory
process described above was developed in an experimental group at
Post Graduate Center, New York City, in 1980. The process models
an atmosphere and attitude which can soon resonate throughout the

therapeutic chain, thereby lifting staff morale, engendering peer support and building feelings of confidence and esteem.

Briefly outlined the main principles of conducting this type of group are (1) Open listening, and focusing, (2) The group leader as a model, (3) An anxiety-free and accepting atmosphere, (4) "The resolution experience."[1]

Intrinsic to all four principles are the techniques of group process. The group becomes the instrument through which teaching and learning are established and promoted.[6,7] The richness of the process helps the group members move closer to both a collective and individual understanding of their patients as well as their own inner experiences. The group process allows a greater acknowledgement of and appreciation for each group member as well as an arena to reflect on the fact that the therapist or the group leader does not have all the answers. The group then becomes one of the most important modes of learning and problem solving. Each member comes to feel that s/he has had a personal and active participation in the creation of this learning process. The importance of this can carry over into our group work with our alcoholic patients.

OPEN LISTENING AND FOCUSING

The hallmark of active listening and focusing is that the focus must be directly on the emerging needs of the presenter (i.e., the person choosing to present a problem for the supervisory group). Before the group attends to the manifest issues specific to the presenter's patient or group, it holds its focus on the identification of the presenter's need for bringing in the problem. When this focus is maintained, the nature of the conflict which created the problem becomes clarified. Therefore, the group listens to the exact words being used, asking when necessary, "Let me see if I heard you correctly" and repeating the exact words used.[1] In the case material presented here, only when the group leader referred to A's exact words did a new avenue open up for understanding his conflict.

We also focus on the effect the presenter's material has on the group as a whole and on each group member. Only when the presenter expresses satisfaction verbally or by some other bodily movement (often a smile) do we know that his or her supervisory need has been fully understood. The fact that *only* the presenter can be the final judge of the accuracy of the focusing helps to make the group a safer place. When the group members reflect back to the presenter an appreciation of his or her conflict and an understanding of what has been presented, the presenter no longer feels stuck and alone with the problem.

THE GROUP LEADER AS MODEL

The supervisory leader's presence and actions are crucial. The leader's attitude needs to be genuine, conveying a caring and sense of appreciation and dignity for each group member and the group as a whole. With "open listening,"[6,7] the leader attempts to suspend any theoretical framework, listening as free as possible of judgment and explanations. The leader's attitude includes a trust in the rich life experience of each group member.

The leader gently guides and firmly holds the boundaries of focus on the problem being presented. Manipulative, hostile, and tangential responses are understood as reflections on the "parallel process." All responses are considered important and are encouraged. The discussion is constantly retraced to where it belongs—the discovery of the feelings about the patient or group. The focus is always on how the presenter *felt* when with the patient or group, how the supervisory group members *felt* when listening to the presenter, what were the feelings prompting the hostile response, etc. The leader constantly returns to the boundaries of the task, revealing how the problem of the presenter, and his or her patient or group are a common problem for all of the group members. Clear boundaries are maintained between supervisory work and personal therapy. The clarity of the boundaries and the protection against personal hostility lessen the anxiety in the group and permit greater empathic responsiveness. With this model, interpretation is rare.

ANXIETY FREE AND ACCEPTING ATMOSPHERE

The establishment of an anxiety-free and accepting atmosphere is "characterized by a pervasive group attitude of caring."[1] Each group member comes to trust in a non-judgmental uncritical, gentle, supportive, "holding environment."[15] Inherent in this attitude is an appreciation of and sense of value for each person; respect and awareness that all have resistance, defenses and conflict. With the focus on mutual help and learning a collective exploratory process evolves. Uncertainty is invited. Compassion, curiosity and self awareness replace hostility, competition, criticism, and other types of self defense. The case material above indicates the beginning of this process in the group.

THE RESOLUTION EXPERIENCE

"The resolution experience" is an experiential state in which the presenter feels genuinely helped, cared about, no longer alone, and understood on profound levels. While the focus remains on the presenter, "the resolution experience" is shared by all the group members through their emotional identification with the presenter. There is usually a deep collective feeling of group unity, freedom and joy. This state of resolution is delicate but not fragile. Each member must either join in or at a minimum not interfere in the process. "The resolution experience" does not occur in every session; however, there is a tenacity in the group's effort toward the experience, and the more a group works together the more often it can occur.

The group supervisory leader encourages the group to stay with the experience long enough for it to be felt and recognized by all the members. The next step in the process is the presenter's verbalization of feeling helped. Often s/he refers "back to the problem with new insight, renewed energy, and new ideas regarding ways of working through the problem."[1] Often responses of group members which were rejected earlier in the process are now understood and appreciated. Learning that occurs during this process is experienced through the entire "chain" of supervisory contact, i.e., supervisor to therapist and group members to patients.[5] Thus, as in our case example, a therapist who is discouraged with his alcoholic patient can bring this to the group and develop a renewed sense of commitment and hope.

SUMMARY

The authors have described and discussed some of the concepts and causes of burnout and countertransference in working with alcoholic patients. Clinical excerpts have been offered which elluci- date these phenomena and illustrate a supervisory group process approach to mediating these feelings and using them to help our patients and supervisees. The paper concludes with a brief outline of the principles involved in this interactional focused listening group process.

REFERENCES

1. Angel, V., Katz, C., et al. "Principles in Analytic Group Supervision to Leaders Who Supervise Therapists Using a Group Process Modality." *Group and Family*. New York. Bruner Mazel, Aronson & Wolberg, Eds., 1983.

2. Daley, M. R. "Burnout: Smoldering Problem in Protective Services." *National Association of Social Workers*, 1979, pp. 375-379.

3. Doehrman, M. & Gross, J. "Parallel Process in Supervision and Psychotherapy." *Bulletin of the Menninger Clinic*, Vol. 40, No. 1, January, 1976.

4. Edelwich, J. & Brodsky, A. *Burn-Out: Stages of Disillusionment in the Helping Professions*. Human Science Press, 1980.

5. Ekstein, P. & Wallerstein, R. *The Teaching and Learning of Psychotherapy* (ed. 2). New York, International Universities Press, 1972.

6. Fielding, B. "Focusing in Dynamic Short Term Therapy: Three Case Studies." *Colloquium*, New York, Vol. 2. pp. 64-78, June, 1979.

7. Fielding, B. "Group Supervision: The Interaction of Therapists and Supervisors That Facilitates and Hinders Learning in a Group." *Colloquium*. New York, Vol. 2 & 3. December, 1979 and June, 1980.

8. Freudenberger, H.J. *Burn-Out—How To Beat The High Cost of Success*. New York. Bantam Books, 1980.

9. Gottheil, E. "Attitudinal Factors and Staff Morale." *Alcoholism Counselor Burnout Symposium*, State of New York, Division of Alcoholism and Alcohol Abuse. July, 1980 (unpublished paper).

10. Pines, A. & Maslach, C. "Characteristics of Staff Burnout in Mental Health Settings." *Hospital and Community Psychiatry*, Vol. 29, No. 4, pp. 233-237, April, 1978.

11. Racker, H. *Transference and Countertransference*. New York, International Universities Press, 1968.

12. Rogers, C. R. *On Becoming A Person*, Boston, Houghton Mifflin, 1961.

13. Tamerin, J. "Countertransference Issues in the Psychotherapy of Hospitalized Alcoholics," presented at New York City Affiliate, *National Council on Alcoholism Training Session*, April, 1981 (unpublished paper).

14. Wallace, J. "Burnout: An Overview." *Alcoholism Counselor Burnout Symposium*, State of New York Division of Alcoholism and Alcohol Abuse, July, 1980.

15. Winnicott, D. *The Maturational Process and the Facilitating Environment: Studies in the Theory of Emotional Development*, New York, International Universities Press, 1965.

16. Yalom, E. D. *The Theory and Practice of Group Psychotherapy*, New York, Basic Books, 1970.

APPENDIX A
Principles in Effective Listening
(All principles are mutually interdependent)

A. Focusing

   1. Focus on *why* the supervisee (presenter) is in conflict before attending to the manifest content.

2. Listen to the *exact* words being used. Clarify if necessary, e.g., "Let me see if I heard you correctly," followed by repeating the exact words.
3. Focus on the *effect* the presentation has on the group, and on each group member.
4. When the focus is maintained the nature of the conflict becomes clarified.
5. The sharper the focus the closer we are to the inner experience of the patient(s).
6. The full meaning can only be known when the presenter shows satisfaction (verbally or by some bodily movement, e.g., a smile). Only the presenter is the final judge of the accuracy of the focusing. (This also helps to create a safe atmosphere.)

B. An Accepting Atmosphere
   1. A place where uncertainty is invited.
   2. A caring and nurturing place.
   3. The atmosphere needs to be as anxiety-free as possible.
   4. A non-critical, non-judgmental, gentle, supportive "holding" environment.
   5. An appreciation for and valuing of every person.
   6. An awareness and respect for all to have defenses, resistances and conflict.
   7. A sense of collective concern and helping.

C. The Group Leader: A Model of "Open Listening"
   1. A genuine attitude.
   2. Speak and listen softly.
   3. Convey a special caring and sense of appreciation and dignity for the group and each group member.
   4. A suspension of theoretical frameworks and listening largely free of judgments and predisposed explanations.
   5. A trust in the life experiences of the group members and self.

D. "The Resolution Experience"
   1. An experiential state in which the presenter feels genuinely helped, cared about, no longer alone, unencumbered and understood on profound levels.
   2. This state is delicate but not fragile—it can be approached and reapproached many times. There is a tenacity in the group's efforts toward resolution.

3. The delicacy comes from a vulnerability due to a reduction in defensive activity and feelings of heightened intimacy.
4. The group leader encourages the group members to stay with the experience long enough for it to be recognized and felt.